Positive Parenting

Positive parenting is a series of handbooks primarily written for parents, in a clear, accessible style, giving practical information, sound advice and sources of specialist and general help. Based on the authors' extensive professional and personal experience, they cover a wide range of topics and provide an invaluable source of encouragement and information to all who are involved in child care in the home and in the community.

Other books in this series include:

Talking and your child 0 340 57526 3 by Clare Shaw – a guide outlining the details of how speech and language develops from birth to age 11 and how parents can help with the process.

Your child from 5–11 0 340 54750 2 by Jennie and Lance Lindon – a guide showing parents how they can help their children through these crucial early years, stressing the contribution a caring family can make to the emotional, physical and intellectual development of the child.

Help your child through school 0 340 60796 3 by Jennie and Lance Lindon – a guide which looks at the school years from the perspective of the family, showing how parents can help their children to get the most out of their years at primary school and how to ease the transition into secondary education.

Help your child with maths 0 340 60767 X by Sue Atkinson – a comprehensive guide to show parents how they can help develop their children's mathematical awareness and confidence from babyhood through the primary years and into secondary school.

Help your child with reading and writing 0 340 60768 8 by Lesley Clark – a guide which describes the stages children go through when learning to read and write and shows parents how they can encourage and enjoy their children's early development in these vital areas.

Prepare your child for school 0 340 60797 1 by Clare Shaw – a very practical guide for parents whose children are about to start school.

Help your child with a foreign language 0 340 60766 1 by Opal Dunn – written for all parents, including those who do not speak a foreign language, this guide examines the right time to start teaching a child a foreign language, how to begin, and how to progress to fluency.

Teenagers in the family 0 340 62106 0 by Debi Roker and John Coleman of the Trust for Adolescence covers all the major issues that parents face as their children pass through the turbulent teenage years, such as rules and regulations, setting boundaries, communication, decision making, risky behaviour, health issues, and problems at school.

Teenagers and sexuality 0 340 62105 2 by John Coleman of the Trust for Adolescence gives practical advice for parents who are finding it difficult to talk to their teenagers about sex and who need help to understand, and deal with, their teenagers' emerging sexuality.

Help your child with homework and exams 0 340 65866 5 by Jennie Lindon offers parents practical advice on how they can help their children to take a positive approach to homework and exams across the whole school curriculum.

Help your child be confident 0 340 67004 5 by Clare Shaw is packed full of ideas for parents on how to build their children's confidence, ensuring that children grow up feeling good about themselves and the world around them.

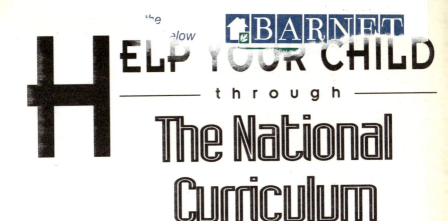

ELP YOUR CHILD

through

The National Curriculum

A PARENTS' HANDBOOK

Graeme Kent

eadway · Hodder & Stoughton

British Library Cataloguing in Publication Data

Kent, Graeme, 1933–
  Help your child through the National Curriculum. – (Positive parenting)
  1. Home schooling – England   2. Education, Elementary – Parent participation –
England
  I. Title
  649.6'8'0942

ISBN 0 340 669365

First published 1996
Impression number 10 9 8 7 6 5 4 3 2 1
Year   1999   1998   1997   1996

Typeset by Wearset, Boldon, Tyne and Wear
Printed in Great Britain for Hodder & Stoughton Educational, a division of Hodder
Headline Plc, 338 Euston Road, London NW1 3BH by Cox & Wyman Ltd,
Reading, Berks.

About the author

Graeme Kent has taught in many primary schools at home and overseas. For eighteen years he was headteacher of St Thomas' Primary School in Boston, Lincs. This was described in the *Independent on Sunday's* selection of Britain's best schools as 'a quite remarkable primary school that seemingly manages to involve everybody – parents, teachers, governors, support staff, local authority councillors – in a drive to get the best for their pupils.' He has written a number of textbooks and books on education, as well as twelve novels. He is the father of two children.

Acknowledgments

My thanks to the teachers, parents and children of Freshwater Primary School, Isle of Wight, Church Street Junior School, Portsmouth and St Thomas' Primary School, Boston, from whom I learnt so much and to whom I owe even more.

The Publishers would like to thank the children of Charlbury Primary School, Oxfordshire, for their help with the covers for this series.

Contents

*To my wife Janet, whom I watched with love and admiration
as she taught and nurtured our two children,
even in the jungles of the Solomon Islands!*

CHAPTER ONE

Introduction

Helping your child with the National Curriculum

The school's really keen on involving the parents. I only went in to deliver my son's lunch-box and I ended up as secretary of the PTA and coach to the netball team!

You do not have to be a trained teacher to help your child at home with the National Curriculum. As a parent, what you are best at is guiding and helping your child at an individual level. By following a few basic guidelines it is possible to give your child a really useful and practical supplement to what she is being taught in the classroom. By working with her in this way you can both enjoy one another's company and have quality time together.

Today, more than ever, education is a partnership between home and school. By steering your child in the right direction at home you can give her the confidence and the ability to make the most of what she is learning at school. Do not be afraid that you will upset your child's teachers. In today's busy climate schools actively welcome all the help they can get from home. This book is intended to help you provide that help and to give you and your child a good time together in the process.

The introduction of the National Curriculum means that the same basic educational material is being taught and tested in all state primary schools. This makes it a lot easier for parents to help and build on the foundations provided by the school, and makes it less traumatic if a family has to move to another area.

Your child at school

For six years at primary school your child will follow the guidelines provided by the National Curriculum in nine subjects. Twice during that period, at the ages of seven and eleven, she will take National Assessment Tests in English, mathematics and science.

Throughout her primary school years your child will almost certainly be taught with care and devotion by dedicated teachers. However, there is one thing which even the best of teachers can not give your child – sufficient time. *You* can provide the essential individual attention which will build on the work of the school. Your child should respond to the patience you can bring to bear on her problems and, in a one-to-one situation with no other children to laugh at her, ought not to be shy about telling you if there is something she does not understand.

The subjects of the National Curriculum

Between the ages of five and eleven children have to be taught three **core** subjects and six **foundation** subjects, as set out below:

Core subjects: English, mathematics and science (and Welsh in Welsh-speaking schools)
Foundation subjects: history, geography, art, music, design and technology and physical education

As far as religious education is concerned, children must follow a religious education syllabus. These are devised locally by special committees. They are mainly Christian in content but also take into account the teachings and practices of the other principal religions represented in Great Britain.

INTRODUCTION

Age divisions

In primary schools the National Curriculum subjects are taught at two levels. These are Key Stage 1 and Key Stage 2. In most schools Key Stage 1 is taught at the infant stage (five- to seven-year-olds) and Key Stage 2 is taught to junior school children (those between the ages of seven and eleven).

Home–school liaison

Most primary schools go to great lengths to keep in touch with parents and to let them know what is going on. It will be of the greatest benefit to your child if you take every chance to respond to these initiatives. Your child's teacher will constantly be assessing her progress and letting you know how she is getting on at school. In particular she will be constantly assessing her progress in the subjects of the National Curriculum and talking to you about this.

When it comes to helping your child through the National Curriculum the first and most important thing that you should do is to establish a good relationship with your child's teacher at the beginning of each school year. This should not be difficult. Primary schools today are desperately keen to involve parents in the running of the schools. Schools are responsible to the parents and the community they serve, and are well aware of this fact. If they are not, parents will soon vote with their feet and take their children elsewhere.

Every state school has a number of parent-governors eager to act as representatives of other parents. All sorts of moves are under way in schools to let parents know what is going on – brochures, newsletters, open meetings, and so on. Schools are also inspected regularly, and one of the first things that the inspectors will want to know is how happy the parents are with the way they are being involved. They will even hold a special meeting before the inspection just for this purpose. This means that there should be a receptive climate for any overtures you want to make in an effort to help *your* school educate *your* child. If you approach the teacher pleasantly at the right time, with a genuine desire to make a friend and ally of her, you will find that your interest will be appreciated and that you will be met more than half-way.

By far the best time to make your first approach is at the first open evening organised by the school at the beginning of the school year in the Autumn term, when your child is new to the class. All schools have to hold these meetings to let you know how your child is settling in and to answer any questions you may have about her. Sometimes these meetings are held quite late in the term, but this is not a bad thing as it means that the teacher has had a chance to get to know the children in her care and also to be able to adapt her teaching plans for the year according to the needs and capabilities of her new class.

Do not make any effort to help with teaching activities until you have met the teacher at this open evening. This will give you a rest and your child a chance to adapt to all the new things which will be happening to her. After you have had your chat with the teacher there will be at least two terms and a bit for you to provide your input, and this will give you plenty of time each year.

When the day comes for you to see the teacher, if your child enjoys being in her class, tell her so and add how glad you are that she is in her care. Reassure her by your approach and attitude that you are not an interfering parent, and that all you want to do is back her up in anything that she is doing. Ask her if she wants to talk to you then and there about how you can help, or whether she would rather you made an appointment to see her individually at a less busy time.

Whatever time you arrange between you, say that you want to reinforce what she is doing and ask her if she has any specific suggestions. You should find that any areas where you are asked to help are covered in one of the chapters of this book, with suggestions as to how you can also follow the course of the National Curriculum at home.

With the best will in the world misunderstandings will arise between home and school and parent and child. With the use of common sense on all sides these can be sorted out and even be used to the advantage of all concerned. An example of such an occasion was when one five-year-old girl burst into tears on a car journey through the countryside with her mother. When asked what was wrong, the girl sobbed, 'Teacher told us all to look for signs of spring, but all I can see are signs saying "No Entry!" and "Major Road Ahead!" '

However, true to the great traditions of home–school co-operation, when the mother explained what had happened, the teacher of Year 6 used this confusion to get her class to combine to write a poem on the subject:

The signs of spring

I've seen so many signs along the highway,
That show me almost every single thing
From 'Castle' to 'Road Narrows' and 'No Byway',
But I haven't seen a single sign of spring.

The pictures on the signs are really funny,
Traffic lights, and white arrows inside shields.
Has the sign that I want got a bunny
Scampering like a rocket over fields?

Teacher says I should find signs of spring near,
I've looked and looked, but all that I can see
Are lambs and flowers and little birds that sing here
But where those wretched signs are sure beats me!

Problems

❝ *I have tried to make contact with my child's class teacher and ask how I can help at home, but it is like running into a brick wall. She doesn't seem to want to have anything to do with parents.* ❞

Gone are the days when schools put up signs at the gate saying 'No parents past this point!' Schools now *want* to involve parents, or they should do. The whole point of the Parents' Charter is that schools must be accountable to parents. The charter lays down a number of ways in which schools should tell parents what they are doing and how they can help.

If you are having difficulty in establishing contact it is likely to be the fault of one particular teacher. She may be too set in her ways, or just shy and find it difficult to relate to other adults, but be very good with the children. Talk to other parents about her and find out how they manage to get through to her. If they say that they also find it hard to establish a relationship with the teacher then you really should take it further. Your child's time in a class is too short and too precious for any of it to be conducted in a divided 'us' and 'them' situation. Have an informal word with the headteacher. See if she can suggest anything. If this does not work then ask one of the parent governors to bring the matter up at the next governors' meeting.

After all this, if nothing happens, then you will really have to ask yourself whether the other aspects of the school are so good that they outweigh the manner in which the parents are being frozen out. If they are not, then there are other primary schools who will be only too pleased to take your child. This, of course, should be the very last resort.

Using this book

Each chapter is devoted to a different age level, starting with Year 1, when your child will be five or six, and going on to Year 6, the final year in the primary school, when your child will be eleven. There are also chapters devoted to the two national tests at ages seven and eleven. You will find that the terms 'he' and 'she' are used in alternate chapters.

Children do not develop at the same rate, so if you find the activities of one chapter too easy for your child, go on to those in the next chapter. This kind of individual assessment and progression is exactly what the teacher at school is expected to be doing with her children under the terms of the National Curriculum. At the same time, do not worry if your child seems to be falling short of the standards required in any given year. Children progress in fits and starts. A boy or girl who may seem to be a little below average one year may make enormous strides over the next twelve months. If you have any worries or doubts about this consult the teacher. If you do not want to wait until the next open evening drop her a note and ask if you can come in and talk to her. However, there is little point in doing this until close to the end of the year, because of the uneven progress children make at this age.

In each year of the National Curriculum in the primary school there are certain aspects of each subject which are particularly important for your child to master if she is to make progress. These special areas are covered in the different chapters.

When should I help my child?

The educational activities designed here are intended to be interesting and pleasurable for both you and your child. She should enjoy taking part in them and you should have the satisfaction of watching her grow and develop.

If you already set aside time to talk and play games with your child, use this time for the activities suggested. At both infant and junior school stages they should be just as much fun and rather more educationally slanted. If you are not in the habit of setting aside a specific time to be with your child, then try to spend fifteen to twenty minutes over the activities together two or three times a week in Years 1 and 2, and about half an hour at a time for Years 3 to 6. If your child is too tired or not interested some evenings, put aside a special time at the weekends and in the school holidays.

No parent would want or be able to duplicate all the aspects of the National Curriculum at home, but by choosing from the activities suggested in this book you will be able to build upon and enhance the education being provided at school and to show your child that education is an on-going affair, not bounded by the walls of a classroom.

Throughout the book you will find more activities than you can complete in the different subjects. This is to give you an element of choice and to enable you to fit in with what is being taught at school and to help your child with any aspects of a subject with which she is uncertain. Pick and mix as you feel fit, it is all grist to the mill. Even with an older child do not spend more than half an hour a day on any of the activities. Some days give them a miss completely. If she is really interested she may go off on her own and carry on with what has been started.

Your child will benefit enormously if you take an informed interest in her work and let her know that you are always there to help. Education is an on-going process, not confined to a classroom. Your child will discover this in the best possible way if she sees that you want her to achieve her maximum potential and that she can carry on the learning process at home if and when she wants to, without any pressure being applied.

Look at her school books when she brings them home, and talk to her about what she is doing. If she sees that you value the work she is doing at school then she will value it even more and want to share her school activities with you. If she knows that she can talk about her learning problems in a calm and supportive way with you then she will be all the more willing to bring her difficulties to you. Give her the confidence of knowing that at school or at home there is always someone wanting and able to help her.

With a younger child a simple 'What did you do at school today?' is often enough for her to talk about her activities. Once your child has reached the junior school, however, she may at first be less willing to talk about her other world, but after Year 3 there is generally a change of attitude, especially when the work gets harder and she is hoping for help from home! Look for ways in which to comment in a complimentary way about the books and projects that she brings home. Let her see that you are interested and want to share with her.

The key to helping at home is *relaxation*. Do not make a big thing about doing curriculum work at home. Like all of us, children like doing what they are good at, and you can help your child to become as good at her work as it is possible for her to be. Show by your own low-key attitude that it is the most natural thing in the world for education to be as much a part of her home environment as eating, sleeping and playing. A good primary school will also do its share to make your child feel that you are an important part of her education.

Books and equipment

Educational toys and a wide range of suitable reading books will be of great help to home teaching if they are well chosen and properly used. Each chapter has a list of suggested aids for the age range being discussed.

The National Curriculum stresses the importance of information technology in all subjects, so playing computer games and taking part in any other forms of IT will also assist your child, but plenty of time will be devoted to this at school in the junior stage and even more when your child goes on to secondary education, so don't worry if you do not have a computer at home.

Parents talking

❝ I could see that the teacher didn't know whose mum I was, but she didn't want to admit it. She kept on talking, hoping I would give her some sort of clue, but I wouldn't. It became a battle of wills between us. In the end she had to admit that she had no idea who I was. We got on fine after that. Teachers aren't infallible – neither are parents! ❞

CHAPTER TWO

Year 1 – ages five to six

> *I don't mind my five-year-old adding up faster than I can, but I just wish she wouldn't be so smug about it!*

By the time your child reaches the first year of the National Curriculum he will probably already have spent a year in the reception class at school and will have been taught the rudiments of reading, writing and number. The National Curriculum is designed to build on these foundations, slowly at first and then in increasing detail. From time to time the teacher will revise what has been learnt earlier in the school, in order to make sure that your child has not forgotten anything important.

Throughout this year the school will be concentrating mainly on teaching your child the basics of English and mathematics, with a little elementary science. Often the other subjects will be grouped in what are called 'cross-curricular' projects, blending them in together. Look at the Key Stage 2 project on 'Homes' to see how an everyday topic can cover all the different subjects.

This is certainly a method which you could use during Key Stage 1 with your child. If he has a particular interest in horses, for example, this could be used as the basis for all sorts of useful curriculum work – looking for stories (English), finding out how a horse is cared for (science), collecting pictures and trying to draw horses (art), making lists of animals which move faster or slower than horses (mathematics), reading about horses of the past, (history), and so on.

A Key Stage 2 project on homes

English
Write a story about your home and some of the people in it. Find stories and poems about homes, like *Cinderella*, and *The old woman who lived in a shoe.*

History
How long have you lived in your home? Ask your parents what happened the day they moved in.

Science
Make a list of some of the homes animals live in. Draw pictures of them.

Geography
Where is your home? Draw a map showing how to get there from your school.

HOMES

Art
Draw a picture of the sort of home you would like to live in.

Design and technology
Make a model of a bird's nest out of string and pieces of cloth.

Religious education
Read the story of Noah and his Ark. Why did he build his new home?

Maths
Count the number of doors, windows, steps, chairs and beds in your house.

Other projects which appeal to children of this age include transport, animals, food, holidays, friends, giants, etc.

At school the busy teacher will eagerly be looking for help with all the activities she is undertaking. To help her she will use classroom ancillaries, parents who can come in for an hour a day, or one or two days a week, and all sorts of other volunteers. If she also realises that you are following up her work and reinforcing it at home she will know that your child has a real chance of getting the most from his education.

Let your child's teacher know at your first open evening meeting that you want to help, and go through with her the special areas where she thinks your child could do with assistance. Then use the particular sections in these chapters to help you cover the areas you have chosen. If the teacher says, as she may well do, that any help you give at home will be appreciated, but does not give you any concrete suggestions, then select some of the activities from different subjects and work through these with your child.

You will probably find that the teacher will want to keep in touch with you about the help you are providing at home. Most of them will welcome the chance for a chat about your child's progress if you drop in after school when you pick your child up. Do not do this too often, the teacher will have thirty or so other parents who need her help and advice, but once or twice a term will be fine.

National Curriculum English

During this year at school your child's teacher will start the National Curriculum course by trying to develop in him

- a love of reading and the ability and desire to explore books and stories for himself;
- the ability to communicate effectively in speech and writing and, equally important, to listen with understanding.

In most schools about five or six hours a week will usually be devoted to the teaching and learning of English in this and subsequent years.

Helping with reading, speaking and listening

Young children usually want to copy and please their parents. It will help your child considerably to develop as a reader if he sees you reading both for pleasure – books, newspapers and magazines; and for instruction – labels, recipes, television listings, manuals, and so on. If there are plenty of books and magazines in the house your child will accept them as an important and even essential part of life.

Building up a home library

Read regularly to your child at home, either books you have chosen yourself or those sent home by the school. Take him along to the children's section of your local public library and show him just how many books there are waiting to be read. Let him select his own books from the library and take them home.

Select a specific time for reading each day, perhaps just before your child goes to bed, so that he looks forward to your exclusive company. Make your child a part of the reading experience by cuddling him, showing him the pictures and discussing the story and the illustrations. Establish ground rules – that your child listens while you are reading and then talks to you afterwards. Discuss the stories with your child and encourage him to express his own feelings about the stories and characters.

As you read with your child try to immerse yourselves in the story, discussing the events in it, so that he will start thinking about the plot and characters and not just be a passive listener. Good questions at this stage are 'Why did he do that, do you think?' 'Was that a sensible thing to do?' 'What do you think will happen next?', and so on.

Look for books which are attractive in appearance, with bright colours and striking illustrations. At this stage you are 'selling' a love of reading to your child and you have got to make the product look attractive.

After a time your child should show a preference for certain books and will want to look at them himself, perhaps on his own. He may have certain interests – animals, witches, and so on. Don't worry if he seems to select themes and illustrations which do not appeal to you so much. Your child will be exercising his judgement and developing his personal tastes. Ask him why he has chosen a certain book; you may find the answers interesting and it will develop your knowledge of him even further.

By using your library and local book shops try to show him that there is nothing that cannot be had from a book. It is just a matter of searching for the right one. Take him with you when you visit the libraries and shops and let him see you selecting and rejecting books for yourself. This is a very important development and should be encouraged. If your child becomes sufficiently motivated and interested in books at this stage he will want to read for himself and this will hasten the whole reading process.

At this age begin to collect some of the 'classics' for young children. These could include the fairy tales of Joseph Jacobs – *Dick Whittington, Jack and the Beanstalk*, etc.; the tales of Charles Perrault, which include *Cinderella*; *Aesop's Fables*; and the tales of Hans Anderson, all in suitably simplified and well-illustrated versions. Children of this age also enjoy nursery rhymes. They can read these aloud and so develop a feeling for the sound and rhythm of language.

Encourage your child to feel that these are 'his' books, his own personal property, and that he is responsible for keeping them together and looking after them. Let him have a box or bookcase for this purpose.

Problems

> ❛ My five-year-old much prefers looking at comics to reading books. Is this a bad thing, and can I do anything about it? ❜

Within reason encourage your child to read anything at this stage. Obviously you will not let him come into contact with illustrations which will frighten or disturb him, but if he wants to look at the pictures in *Topper* or any other comic this is fine, especially if he will talk about the pictures with you.

Every so often some chief librarian or educational guru will condemn the writings of Enid Blyton, for example, but many parents have good cause to bless the lady's name when their children refuse to read anything but the *Secret Seven* adventures. At least they were still reading for pleasure and maintaining the habit of looking at books. Time enough to go on to other books later.

Identifying with characters

Your child will develop a deeper interest in books and reading if you encourage him to identify with the characters in the books he likes. Encourage him to think about this, and then to come back and talk to you about it. Let him prattle on. The more enthusiastic he seems about what he has read the better the job you are doing as his helper and guide at home.

There are various ways in which you can involve your child personally in the stories he is reading. Encourage him to feel that he is the central character he is reading about and has to deal with the same problems as the ones faced up to in the books. At this age characters in books often seem more real to children than the real-life sporting and pop-star heroes they will idolise a little later in life.

Responding to a story

Discuss the story with your child. Ask 'What is the story about?' 'Who is in it?' Jog your child's memory by going through the illustrations with him and asking him what they are about. Encourage him to discuss the problems faced by the main character. Ask, 'What would you do if you were that person?' Help your child by going through the main points of the story without the aid of the illustrations, agreeing between you on the problems faced by the leading character.

You can also use favourite stories for all sorts of jumping-off points which should help make the story come to life in your child's mind. Combining books and the 'real' world in this way will stimulate his imagination and encourage him to approach stories with a lively and enquiring mind.

The Story of Tom Thumb – the Brothers Grimm

The main problem in this story is that Tom never grew to be bigger than a person's thumb, which is how he gained his name.

- Make a collection of objects about as big as a man's thumb. Display your collection on a table and talk about the different objects. Could he have been named after one of these – Tom Nail, Tom Thimble, etc?
- Tom hid in an empty snail shell and then in a mouse hole. Where could you hide in your house if you were Tom's size? Make a model of Tom out of modelling clay and look for places in which to hide him.
- What household objects could you use if you were Tom's size? You might be able to use a needle as a sword, a cotton-reel for a table, etc. Make a collection of things you could use and discuss them.
- What would be the advantages and disadvantages of being Tom's size?
- Whatever he looked like, Tom's parents always loved him. How would this help him?

Other stories which can be used as springboards for all sorts of follow-up activities include *The Tinder Box; The Fir Tree; Snow White and the Seven Dwarfs;* and *Cinderella.*

Giving and following instructions

When you are out with your child, quietly point out examples of people giving instructions to others. If someone in the supermarket is overseeing the stacking of shelves by another worker, show your child how important it is that the instructions are clear and accurate and how carefully (hopefully) the stacker is listening to the supervisor. Show your child traffic lights and pedestrian crossings and explain how important it is to follow the right instructions when crossing the road.

Your child will soon learn the benefits of listening carefully if you both play a series of games involving giving and responding to instructions. These could start by a simple game of 'Simon Says!', when the child only obeys if a command is prefaced by the words *'Simon Says!'* You can then go on to games of 'Hot and Cold' where you hide something in the room and ask your child to look for it. When he gets close to the object say 'Hot!', and when he is far from it, say 'Cold!'

After a few weeks he should be ready to respond to more detailed instructions. Ask him to imagine that he is a robot, following instructions as he is 'programmed' to move about a room: 'Four paces forward ... two paces to the left ... three paces forward ...' etc. Reverse the roles and ask him to give you instructions while you respond.

Work together in the kitchen following a simple recipe. Read aloud the instructions and assemble the ingredients and start cooking them. Let him see exercise videos in which people move in response to the instructions of the trainer.

Writing

In order to get your child going on the National Curriculum his teacher will always be looking for ways of encouraging him to express himself in writing and using his developing skills in this area. She will encourage him to:

- react to stories;
- communicate feelings;
- keep diaries;
- recall experiences;
- provide instructions.

Above all she will try to instil in your child the sheer enjoyment of creating and communicating.

Let your child see you writing in as many different ways as possible. Ask him to help you make some of these messages as clear as you can. How many bottles of milk are you going to ask for in the note to the milkman? How are you going to phrase the note so that it is polite as well as clear, using 'please' and 'thank you' as appropriate?

Even at this early stage it is important to put over to your child that his writing must be adapted for different purposes and audiences. If you are sending a postcard to Aunt Jane, it will be written in a different way to a note to the plumber. A story, for example, will be written in a different way to a set of instructions.

Look at examples of different sorts of writing and talk to your child about the differences. What, for example, are the differences between the story of Tom Thumb and the planting instructions on a packet of seeds?

Getting down to it

Encourage your child to write as much and in as many different forms as possible. At first he may be reluctant to get down to what is a fairly new and laborious skill, but with the exercise of patience on both sides it should not be long before he is keen to show you what he can do. Two fifteen-minute periods a week should be plenty of time for this activity. You might need to start with smaller periods of time and work up to the quarter-hour sessions.

Begin each session by going over the correct way to hold a pencil and have a little practice in the formation of letters. Then encourage him to work on his own, with you looking over his shoulder, commenting on the work, making suggestions and providing encouragement. Always have a good supply of soft pencils and paper handy; your child could go off the boil if he has to wait while you assemble the materials.

Making lists

Making lists are a good way to get your child writing on his own, especially if they are linked to his everyday life and needs. Let him see you writing shopping lists, lists of jobs to do about the house, lists of items stored in the attic. Ask him to help you while you compile these lists.

Lists are easy to write for a beginner and will give a child a quick sense of achievement. Go around with your child as he is making the lists, and make suggestions of your own if he seems stuck. Start with lists of useful activities and encourage your child to use them, highlighting the most important entries and ticking them off as they are accomplished. Later on you could go on to more general lists. Some examples are given in the tinted box below:

Make lists of:

- jobs to do today;
- things to be cleaned;
- items to take to the cleaners;
- noises I have heard today;
- my friends;
- my favourite foods;
- my relations;
- things in my room;
- games I play;
- flowers in the garden;
- my favourite television programmes;
- my toys;

- different animals;
- things coloured red; etc.

Writing stories

Watch children's stories and plays on the television with your child. Talk to him about them and make the point that the stories on the television are only another form of the stories he is reading in books. We all enjoy stories. Talk about your own favourite television series and why you like them. If you can find the book of the play or story being shown on television go through this with your child, comparing it with the television version.

Ask your child to write down the outlines of stories you have read together, and what he likes about them. From this encourage him to start making up and writing down his own stories. Ask him, 'What is it going to be about?' 'Where will the story take place?' 'Who is going to be in it?' From this you can go on to encourage your child to write stories based on titles you provide, for example: The sleeping giant, The lost kitten, The old house, etc. Ask him to illustrate his favourite stories.

Preparing instructions

Encourage your child to watch you reading simple instructions aloud and following them, for example, making a cake, or planting seeds from the instructions on the packet. Encourage your child to write down his own basic sets of instructions. Start with real needs, like how to tie up shoelaces and keep a room tidy. Then go on to more general instructions, like how to get from his bedroom to the kitchen, how to make a bed, how to clean his teeth properly, how to play simple games. Ask your child to read his instructions aloud to you while you try to carry them out to see how accurate they are. Discuss any problems in the instructions and how they might have been made clearer.

The mechanics of writing

At this age the teacher will be trying very hard to encourage your child to write freely and in a variety of forms. At the same time she will also be building on the mechanics or basics of writing started in the reception class – handwriting, grammar, and spelling.

Reconciling the two is not easy. On the one hand it is important for your child to want to express himself freely. At the same time he must be taught these basics so that he can make his writing even more effective.

There will never be enough time at school for your child to have sufficient practice in writing, spelling and the basics of grammar, so help from home will be valuable here. As a sympathetic parent you can make these exercises interesting and even fun to do.

Handwriting – lines and circles

Throughout the first year of the infant stage your child will be writing using individual letters. 'Joined-up' writing will come later. All letters are made up of straight lines or circles, or combinations of both. Practise drawing vertical straight lines and circles, trying to keep the circles roughly the same size. Make up games which involve distinguishing between writing '*a*' and '*o*', for example highlight all examples of the letter '*a*' on the page of a newspaper. On another page use a highlighter for all examples of the letter '*o*'.

Vowels and the alphabet

Introduce your child to the shapes of the vowels – *a e i o u*. Practise writing down these letters, at first on their own and then as the central letters of short words – *bag dig dog let bun* etc. You could combine these exercises with creative writing by asking your child to write a short story about a bag, or a dog, etc. Go through the alphabet with him, preferably using cut-out, wooden or magnetic letters which can be handled by your child.

Let him practise writing down the letters of the alphabet, using first lower-case or ordinary letters, and then upper-case or capital letters. Check with the teacher as to how she is teaching her children to shape letters, but at this age most children will be forming letters with the same strokes of the pencil.

Forming lower-case letters

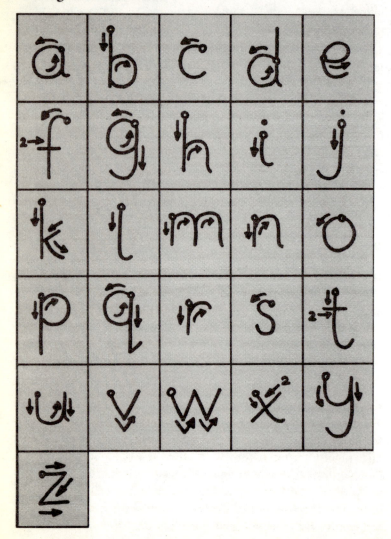

Dictate different letters, for example, *r s a*, and ask your child to write them down, first in the lower-case and then in the upper-case.

Sentences

Your child should begin to understand what a sentence is – a group of words placed in order, so that they make sense. He should also learn that a sentence begins with a capital letter and ends with a full stop, and that all sentences need a *doing* word (verb). This is not an easy idea to grasp, but he will not make much progress with his writing until he can write in complete, sensible sentences.

Help your child to pick out sentences in stories. Point to capital letters and full stops. Ask him to underline or highlight sentences on a page of a magazine or old book. Ask him to make up and say a short sentence. Then ask him to write it down, putting in the capital letter and full stop. Write down the first few words of a sentence and then ask your child to make up and write down two or three words to complete the sentence, putting in the full stop, for example, 'With my hands I can . . .' 'My friend has . . .' etc.

This will be a painstaking business and will need a lot of patience on your part, but it will be worth the effort. Slowly, with your help, your child should begin to recognise and use sentences, a most important part of this section of the National Curriculum.

Spelling

Arouse the interest of your child by asking him to show you how to write down his own name. He will almost certainly have been taught to do this at school and will enjoy displaying his skill. You could ask him to put it at the top of every story or list he writes. Give your child practice in writing down short words beginning with a given letter of the alphabet – *a c f* etc. Begin to write down short words beginning with combinations of letters – *br; la* etc. Write down combinations of short words which rhyme – *land, band; big, dig*, etc.

Problems

> ❛ *My boy just hates the act of writing. He goes all broody if I suggest that he even picks up a pencil!* ❜

This is a common problem. It may be that your child has not mastered the physical aspects of handwriting yet and is unwilling to go through all the bother of trying to form letters. Do not force him. There is plenty of time. At home put him in situations where he might actually see the point of writing and want to do it. He could, for example, work with you on writing invitations to a party, or answer invitations from other children. Give it time.

National Curriculum mathematics

Throughout this year in the mathematics National Curriculum, your child's teacher will be trying to help him to:

- develop an understanding of basic figures;
- use these figures and the 'language' of mathematics, in order to solve simple problems. (The language of mathematics consists of the words used when working with figures – add, take, divide, up, down, etc.)

About five hours a week will usually be set aside for this work.

You can help your child by showing him how important the use of mathematics is to all of us in our everyday lives. Start by letting him hear you use the language of mathematics as a matter of course. If he hears and sees you utilising and employing such terms as: 'how many' 'some' 'all' 'big' 'little' 'top' 'bottom' 'short' 'long' 'full' 'empty' and other mathematical words when you are together, he will become accustomed to them. If he shows an interest, stop to explain and demonstrate them. 'Is this button smaller or bigger than that coin?' 'Which is the biggest apple in this row?', etc.

Comparisons

Making comparisons is an important mathematical concept or idea which can be introduced casually in the home. Play games with your child in which he must guess the sizes of various objects compared with other things. 'Is that vase as big as that cup, or is it smaller?', etc. Show him different items and ask him to rate them in order – big, bigger, biggest, or small, smaller, smallest. Give him something and ask him if it is thinner or fatter than other selected items.

Puppets

Make a number of glove puppets out of old socks. Play simple games with your child in which the puppets respond to simple directions – up, down, top, bottom, left, right, etc. These games could include asking the puppet to wave to the right or left, to fall down, to jump up, and so on.

Reinforce your child's understanding of and interest in numbers by reading him stories concerned with figures such as: *The Two Bears in the Sky; Snow White and the Seven Dwarfs; The Three Little Pigs; The Twelve Passengers.*

Sorting

From making comparisons you can go on to help your child to sort items, by understanding the differences between them. This is a vital basic concept in mathematics and it should be grasped as early as possible.

Play games with your child in which you show him a tray full of different objects: toys, counters, shells, etc. Ask him to sort these groups in different ways. First ask him to sort the articles out by colour – all the red ones, all the green ones, and so on. Then ask your child to sort the items by size – big ones and small ones. Finally ask him to sort the objects by shape – round items and those which are not round. Your child can then go on to sort items by texture, weight, and so on. This will provide an invaluable exercise in discrimination for your child and lay the groundwork for more advanced mathematical activities later on.

Correspondence

Another useful home activity at this age to follow sorting is that of correspondence. This is a more advanced form of sorting and is designed to make your child use his reasoning power and intelligence to work out how things go together. Start by working together on one-to-one correspondence. Give him two piles, with four items in each one. Among the items in each pile should be a square block, of identical shape, size and colour. Your child has to match these two blocks, taking one from each pile. This will show that he can discriminate between the 'like' and the 'different'.

Repeat this process with different piles, making sure that each pile contains one identical object – a ring, a toy, etc. It will be a great help at this stage if you introduce a number of different shapes into your games, so that your child becomes accustomed to seeing and handling squares, circles and triangles. Gradually increase the number of piles in your correspondence games.

At every stage ask your child what he is doing, thus helping him to develop his mathematical vocabulary or language: 'This block is the *same* as that one.' 'That shape is *different*.' Most children enjoy games of this sort and they are of the utmost importance in introducing them to the basics of number work. There is seldom enough time at school for useful activities like these.

Give your child practice with shapes by showing him pictures of squares, triangles, circles and rectangles. Ask him to make 3-D copies of these shapes in modelling clay. Use one piece of clay only and change it from shape to shape to get their 'feel'. Break the shapes into halves and quarters.

Number

After sorting and correspondence activities your child will be ready to go on to number activities, using figures. With a little help from you he should be able, almost unconsciously, to develop an awareness of number, especially with the groundwork you have provided with language, sorting and correspondence games.

Keep emphasising numbers as you play with your child. 'Put *two* blocks on that pile.' 'Show me *three* oranges.' It is essential that your child learns the concept, or general idea, of number before going on to deal with the figures that we use to represent numbers. The school will be devoting a lot of time to this, but there is still plenty that can be done at home to help. Give your child practice with counters, emphasising the numbers as they are placed in piles: '*one* counter here, *two* over there', and so on. Do not go above ten unless you are convinced that he is ready for such progress.

When you believe that your child has grasped the concept of number, go on to reinforce the work with figures which will be taking place at school throughout this period. A good way to do this is to take ten large pieces of white cardboard, each one the same shape and size. On one side of each card draw the figure representing a number from one to ten. On the other side of each card draw a number of coloured dots representing the number on the reverse side. On the back of the number representing 3 there will, of course, be three dots, and so on, up to ten. Play a game regularly with your child involving the use of these cards. Show him the dots on one side of a piece of cardboard, say aloud the number they represent, and then turn the cardboard over, so that he can see the shape of the relevant figure.

After a while show your child a figure and ask him if he can tell you what number it represents. From this go on to show him the side with the number of dots and ask him what number they represent. You could also buy a set of figures from one to ten and let your child handle them and become even more accustomed to them. Some sets of these numbers are magnetic and may be attached to the side of the fridge and displayed by your child to other members of the family as he becomes accustomed to handling them.

Calculators

In Year 1 your child will probably be introduced to calculators in mathematics. There are a number of home activities which you can help him carry out which will help his understanding:

- practise switching on and off;
- make numbers appear and disappear in the window;
- enter familiar numbers –age, house number, etc.;
- fill windows with 2s and count them;
- make patterns in the window – 121212, etc.;
- enter random numbers you call out;
- begin simple addition of digits.

Addition and subtraction

Help your child to count, using concrete objects like counters. Use the same counters for simple addition and taking away. Revise the basic signs + for addition and − for subtraction. He will have been taught these at school, but it is very helpful to reinforce what the school is doing and to make sure that your child understands them.

+ and −

The sign + means *and* or *add.* Give your child practice in adding by asking, 'What does 2 *and* 2 make?' He should be able to say '4'. Then write the sum down, instead of writing '2 and 2', write '2 + 2'. Repeat this with a number of sums until you are sure that he understands that + is a sign for add.

Do the same thing with subtraction or take-away sums. Make sure that your child knows that − is a sign for the word *take* or the words *take away.* The sum 6 take 4, when written down, should look like 6 − 4, and so on. Carry out simple written addition and subtraction activities.

Money

Finally, over the course of this year, begin to introduce your child to money. Take him shopping with you and let him see you paying for your purchases with money, so that he grasps the idea of payment in coins and notes. Let him see and handle different coins. Now and again let him hand over the money in a shop for sweets or ice-cream.

At school the teacher will almost certainly be developing the use of money with your child's class by simulating shops and shopping, with the children buying and selling things, and giving change up to ten pence. This is something you could copy at home. Coins of different sizes and value may be used for sorting activities. Also try giving your child his pocket money in different mixtures of coins. Ask him to count these to make sure that he is getting the correct amount each week.

Problems

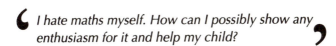

I hate maths myself. How can I possibly show any enthusiasm for it and help my child?

Welcome to the club! If primary teachers had to be adept and enthusiastic at all the subjects they now have to teach the staffrooms of our country would be half empty. You will just have to force yourself! Look on the bright side; at least you are not being expected to teach higher calculus. Take it slowly, keeping one step ahead of your child. I have suggested some useful books to help you at the end of the chapter. You can use the ideas as games but they have been carefully planned to give your infant child plenty of practice in the skills he should be learning at this stage. It is an inescapable fact of parenthood seeing our children gradually outstrip us in ability. With some of us it happens sooner than others.

National Curriculum science

At this stage your child will be encouraged to:

- think in a scientific manner (look for reasons, conduct simple experiments, predict what might happen etc.);
- undertake simple and systematic enquiries into science in everyday life;
- understand about living things;
- understand the different materials around him;
- gain a basic knowledge of such physical processes as electricity, forces and motion and light and sound.

Usually two or three hours a week will be devoted to the teaching of science in Year 1. For most of this time the teacher will be concerned mainly with helping her children to appreciate the environment with all their senses and to arouse their sense of curiosity in the world about them.

You can provide your child with all the back-up he needs for science at this stage on your normal walks together around the house and through the neighbourhood, looking for signs of growth, examining wildlife, noting the signs of the passing seasons, and so on. Throughout the year take every opportunity to introduce your child to the world around him and encourage him to take an interest in that world.

Materials

You can prepare your child at home for the sheer variety of materials around us by giving him a tray containing different objects such as stones, sand, wood and water. Ask your child to feel them and talk about them. In which ways are they the same? How do they differ? Continue to add to the collections over the course of the year.

Growth

Give your child a box of earth and supervise him as he plants seeds, places them in the light and waters them and then watches them grow. These seeds could be planted both in natural surroundings in a garden, or on blotting paper or cotton wool in a glass container. Fast-growing seeds like mustard and cress will present the quickest results. If the seeds come from a packet show your child a picture of the seeds and ask him to compare the picture with the plant when it has grown. Explain that things grow all around us. Encourage him to look at and talk to you about other examples of growing things.

The environment

Take every opportunity to encourage your child to become alert, inquisitive and anxious to learn. Take him for walks to observe the countryside or public parks. Discuss what you see. Explain, with practical examples, how a flower grows, where animals live, where the water in a river comes from, how the countryside changes during the different seasons.

Animals

At this age your child will be too young to be allowed to look after animals on his own. However, if there are any pets in the house encourage him to take an interest in them, observe how they move, what they eat, where they sleep, and so on. Stress that pets depend upon us and that looking after them is an on-going activity.

Caterpillar study

Find a caterpillar and bring it home on the leaf on which you found it.
Cut a supply of similar leaves still on the stem.

Put some soil in the bottom of a glass jar.
Place the leaves and the caterpillar inside the jar.
Keep the stems fresh by placing them in a pot of water inside the jar.
Observe the caterpillar and make notes about what it does.
Draw pictures of what happens.

Other creatures which could be studied in this way include frogs' spawn, worms, etc. Do encourage your child to handle any creatures with care and to return them to their natural habitat after he has studied them.

Sounds

Encourage your child, now and again, to make a list of all the sounds he hears in the course of a day. Put them under different headings: soft sounds; loud sounds; sounds made by people; sounds made by machines, etc. Listen to songs and music together. If he complains that it is too quiet to hear anything encourage him to concentrate by suggesting that you 'listen' to the silence together and see just how many sounds you can really hear.

Vibrations

Give your child a matchbox with an elastic band wrapped around it. Let him pluck the band and listen to the vibration.
Ask him to wet his finger and rub it gently around the stem of a long-stemmed glass. What can he hear?
Ask him to say something, at the same time placing a hand on his throat, to feel the vocal chords moving.
All these sounds have been made by *vibrations* or movements through the air.

Electricity

Try to arouse in your child an understanding that many things around us are powered by electricity, but **never** let your child touch anything electrical at this stage of his development. Take him on a series of walks around the house and show him everything in it which is powered by electricity – lights, bells, television, radio, telephone, etc. Stress the potential dangers of electricity and emphasise the care that adults take when dealing with it.

Making electricity

Provide your child with a hard rubber comb and some woollen cloth. Tear up some paper into small pieces and place them on a table. Ask him to rub the comb with the woollen cloth. This will cause the comb to pick up electrons from the cloth and become charged. Tell your child that by doing this he is making electricity. Ask him to hold the comb close to the pieces of paper and to talk and write about what happens.

The National Curriculum foundation subjects

During Year 1 of the National Curriculum most schools will be concentrating on the core subjects of English, mathematics and science. They must also, however, devote time to what are called the foundation subjects. Most schools will probably try to devote between forty-five and sixty minutes a week to each of these subjects.

National Curriculum design and technology

With a heavy emphasis on safety precautions, your child will be:

- introduced to simple materials, such as wood, stone, plastic, paper, etc.;
- shown how to use simple tools, like paste-brushes, scissors, spreaders, etc.;

- encouraged to design and plan before making anything;
- asked to undertake simple making tasks, like model windmills, paper toys, puppets, etc.

Over the course of the year you can back up the National Curriculum in this subject by letting your child see that useful objects can be planned, made, used and repaired. Take every opportunity of letting him see you getting ready to use tools and then employing them in everyday tasks –mending a washer, replacing a fuse, unblocking a sink, and so on. Talk to your child as you carry out these functions and try to explain exactly what you are doing and why it was important to make preparations and assemble the right tools first. Develop your child's basic technical vocabulary by using such words as flat, round, sharp, twisted, etc. as you work.

Investigations

Help your child to understand how simple mechanisms work by helping him to dismantle old toys. Choose simple wooden models with few parts, for example a motor car with a wooden base, four wheels and perhaps two axles. Do not let him work alone on these projects in case he cuts himself or swallows a component part. Discuss the functions of the different parts as they are revealed. Sort the toys into groups, for example toys which move, toys which do not move, etc.

Loads

Help your child to begin to study design problems and try to solve them. Work out the best ways to carry loads on land and water through various experiments. Operate with a bucket of water, or use a sink or bath, and a number of flat pieces of wood. Float the different pieces of wood in a bowl of water and decide which one would make the most suitable model raft. Then work out the best way to carry a number of coins or other pieces of metal on the raft.

The load must be distributed so that none of it slides off the raft and the raft does not sink under the weight. Experiment with different ways of securing the load and of working out how many coins can be loaded on board before the raft sinks.

Joining

Start to work with tools and materials and select the most appropriate ones for the task in hand. Work with a number of different materials to decide which is the best way to join several pieces of thick cardboard to make a bridge or the walls of a model house or castle. Look at one piece of cardboard and work out whether or not it would be stronger with two pieces joined together. Experiment with paste, glue, paper clips, etc. As always use the appropriate vocabulary as you are working together – thick, thin, strong, join, light, heavy, and so on.

A model snake

Work together to assemble a model snake out of old cotton reels and thick cord. First assemble the snake by joining the cotton reels together by running the cord through the holes. Knot the back end of the cord and pull the snake over the ground by the front end to get an idea of what the completed model will look like. Then take the model to pieces and paint and decorate the individual reels, making the front one the head and the others the body.

National Curriculum history

At this stage your child will be taught little more than to develop an awareness of the past and how it differed from the present. In terms of the National Curriculum the teacher will help your child to:

- study the passing of time;
- distinguish between the past and the present;
- use different ways of looking at the past (books, pictures, etc.);
- look at local history.

History can provide one of the fun aspects of working together at home. Help your child to develop an awareness of the past by concentrating on his own background, reinforcing the idea of the passing of time. Go through photographs of him as a baby, rummage through the attic to find toys he used to play with and compare these with current favourites. Talk about things he did last week, or even last year. Use the concepts *now* and *then*, *past* and *present* as you talk. Discuss birthday parties and what happened at them. Encourage grandparents and other older members of the family to talk about past events in the family.

Just by talking to your child and other members of the family about things you remember which happened weeks, months or even years before, and looking at old photograph albums, you are introducing your child to history and showing him how interesting and useful it can be.

Weather chart

Make a weather chart with your child for each week of the year and put it on the wall, sticking on symbols for the different kinds of weather as they occur – sun, rain, snow, and so on. Over the course of a year discuss how things change as the seasons merge into one another. From time to time look back to see what the weather was like this time last week, or last month and how it compares with the present climate. Continue to use the vocabulary of time – *now, then, last week, last month, a year ago, tomorrow*, etc. This is an on-going project, but need only take a very short time each week. Many children enjoy a long-distance project of this sort, compared with all the other short-term investigations they make at home and school.

Christmas cards

Go through some of the Christmas cards you have received with your child. Pay particular attention to those with traditional pictures of Christmas in the past – stage-coaches, inn scenes, and so on. Compare these pictures with present-day celebrations of Christmas. How do they differ in terms of clothing, transport, etc. Imagine what life was like for a child of your age in those times.

Stories

Read to your child, or allow him to read for himself, simple stories about people who lived in the past. Such stories as Alfred and the cakes, King Arthur and his knights, Noah and his ark should all interest your child and help reinforce in his mind the differences between past and present. He should also be encouraged to read simplified versions of stories concerned with the passing of time, like *Rip Van Winkle*, *The Little Fir Tree*, *The Sleeping Beauty*, and so on.

National Curriculum geography

Children will be encouraged through the National Curriculum to:

- take an interest in their surroundings;
- further their knowledge and understanding of the locality;
- become aware that there is a wider world beyond their own immediate surroundings.

You can help your child at home by helping him to understand that geography is all around us. It can mean a study of the house you live in as much as an investigation of a foreign country. Take every opportunity to take your child for walks and help him to develop an interest in and knowledge of his own neighbourhood.

Show him local parks, supermarkets, etc. Ask him to describe what he can remember about these places and the routes you took to get there. Begin to use the vocabulary of geography – *flat, straight, hill, river, pond, stream,* etc. as you encounter physical features. Compare your locality with other places you visit on holidays or journeys to see relatives and friends.

Geography is one area where television programmes can be of real help. Watch suitable programmes together which show aspects of other parts of the world. Talk about the differences between these areas and your own locality.

A house study

Get your child to go around his house as if he has never seen it before.
What does it look like? How many rooms are there? What are they used for?
Draw pictures of the different rooms.
Make a plan of the whole house.

Using toys

Devise games in which he uses building blocks, etc. to make models of places visited. Collect toy domestic animals and farm machinery to make a model of a farm. As he collects and discards animals talk about their functions on the farm. Why does a farmer keep sheep, cows, pigs, etc.? Why does he not keep lions or elephants as well? Look at the models of farm vehicles. What is the purpose of a tractor? What are the different buildings such as barns used for?

Jobs

Take an interest in the jobs people do and the uniforms that some of them wear – postmen, policemen, nurses, etc. Where do they work? What do they do? What sorts of jobs does your child think he might enjoy one day?

Food and drink

Collect tins and packets from the kitchen. Look at the pictures on them. Some of them will show that the tea, coffee, fruit, etc. came from other countries. Where are these countries? Can you find them on the globe? It is not too soon to have a large, simple map of the world hanging up in your child's bedroom.

National Curriculum art

Children will be encouraged to:

- understand and enjoy art, craft and design;
- express their ideas and feelings;
- record observations;
- design and make artefacts.

You can help your child at home by talking about examples of art around the house – pictures, designs, patterns, etc. Link with geography walks and encourage your child to collect twigs, stones, etc. and to examine them. Discuss the beauty, shape, size and texture of these objects. Ask him to draw his own straight and curved lines with a pencil. Can he put some of those lines together to form a square, etc.?

Patterns

Examine things in the house which have patterns – cups, plates, saucers, wallpaper. Discuss them. Which ones are attractive and which are not? Begin to experiment with different implements and materials – paints, inks, pastels, brushes, crayons, and to devise and create patterns with them.

Illustrations

Look at the illustrations in favourite books. Encourage him to draw his own illustrations for these books.

Art techniques

Experiment with different techniques: paint stones; make friezes from coloured paper; cut up pictures to make small jigsaw puzzles; make mosaic pictures from cut-up gummed paper; create displays of pressed flowers.

National Curriculum music

There are two main segments of the music curriculum:

- performing and composing;
- listening and appraising.

At home, encourage your child to listen to the sounds around him and discuss these. Which sounds does he like and which does he dislike? Do any of these noises seem to have patterns, or *rhythms* which can be anticipated after several hearings? Which of the sounds seem fast and which seem slow? From this he can go on to make and compare his own simple sounds, tearing paper, beating different surfaces, etc. If there are any musical instruments around the house, let the child handle them and work out how sounds may be coaxed from them.

Making instruments

Link with design and technology activities to make and play simple instruments. A tin could be filled with dried peas to make a shaker; a comb covered with tissue-paper can make a primitive mouth organ; different materials stretched across the open mouths of tins can make drums; sandpaper stroked with wooden sticks make raspers, and so on. Let your child make and enjoy his own noises with these instruments.

Composing sounds

As a preamble to composing simple tunes later on, ask your child to imitate sounds he hears. Can he replicate the sound of thunder by beating on a drum? Can he make the sound of a clock ticking by striking a surface with a stick?

Singing

Revise the nursery rhymes and action songs you have learnt and sing them together, sometimes providing an accompaniment with home-made musical instruments. Popular songs at this age include 'Hickory, dickory dock', 'One more river', etc. Encourage sing-songs in the car on long journeys.

National Curriculum physical education

At this stage children will undertake three areas of activity:

- games;
- gymnastics;
- dance.

They may also be taught swimming, but this is often left until later in the school.

It is best to help with physical education in a general way rather than to attempt more specific activities. Play with your child and help him to throw and catch a ball, gently at first and from short distances. Throw the ball in different ways – underarm, rolling along the ground, etc. and then follow it with different movements – walking, running, crawling. Roll the ball at skittles in an attempt to knock them over. Give him practice in using such equipment as hoops, beanbags and rubber rings to help him grow in confidence and ability. Teach him how to skip, first without a rope and then with one. Supervise all your child's physical activities and make sure that they are performed where there is no danger of bumping into things.

Movement

Help your child to move with confidence by playing games in

which you encourage him to move at different speeds in different directions, turning at your command: 'Hop on one leg, slowly, left – go!' 'Walk backwards towards the wall, slowly – go!' Experiment with different ways of jumping, for example, jumping and landing on two feet, jumping on one foot and landing on two feet, etc.

See what balances your child can hold until he begins to feel uncomfortable. 'Stand on your left leg with your right arm outstretched.' 'Crouch down with both hands held out in front of you.'

As your child grows in confidence encourage him to put together sequences of actions – jump, hop, roll, stand. Perform these at different speeds going in different directions. Find ways of travelling on different parts of the body, sliding and rolling.

Swimming

At some time during the infant or junior stage your child will have to learn to swim. The sooner you can get him accustomed to moving in water the better. Take him to the local baths and let him play with you in the shallow end. If he begins to swim, fine; it will help him later on.

Following rules

Help your child to follow rules and play fairly by making sure that when you play games at home you observe the rules of the games.

End of Year 1 checklists

Most, but not all, children should be able to meet the majority of these targets by the end of Year 1.

English

Speaking and listening
The child:

- can talk and listen with increasing confidence;

- is developing a command of detail and vocabulary;
- is listening and responding appropriately to others;
- is beginning to use vocabulary suited to the occasion.

Reading

The child:

- is reading and understanding simple texts;
- is expressing opinions about what has been read.

Writing

The child:

- can communicate in different types of writing – stories, diaries, instructions, accounts, etc.;
- is beginning to write in simple sentences, including using capital letters and full stops;
- is shaping letters consistently;
- is beginning to spell simple words.

Mathematics

The child:

- is beginning to use simple mathematics as an integral part of daily life;
- can count, order, add and subtract to 10;
- can recognise numbers up to 100;
- can recognise simple shapes and work out halves and quarters of these shapes;
- can recognise patterns of numbers and odd and even numbers;
- can sort and classify objects into groups.

Science

The child:

- is beginning to discover and record information;

- is beginning to use simple equipment;
- is beginning to predict what may happen;
- is developing an understanding of living things and their needs;
- is recognising and sorting common materials;
- is developing an awareness of light, sound and movement.

Design and technology

The child:

- is using and understanding simple mechanisms (toys powered by clockwork, elastic, etc.);
- is beginning to identify and use simple tools and techniques to construct objects he has designed;
- understands about loads and stability.

History

The child:

- understands the concept of the passing of time;
- is beginning to understand 'past' and 'present';
- is beginning to look for ways of finding out about the past;
- is developing an understanding of some aspects of the past;
- is beginning to understand why some people in the past acted in the ways they did.

Geography

The child:

- is taking an informed interest in his environment;
- is beginning to take an interest in places outside his immediate locality;
- is selecting information and using observations to ask and respond to questions about places.

Art

The child:

- can record feelings and represent what is seen and touched;
- is choosing resources;
- can describe and compare artefacts;
- can recognise differences in methods and approaches used by artists.

Music

The child:

- can sing songs and play simple pieces;
- can make simple compositions;
- can respond to short pieces of music and compare them.

Physical education

The child:

- is physically active;
- can move well and adopt good posture;
- will try hard and play fairly;
- will follow rules and be mindful of the welfare of others;
- can play simple games;
- can perform simple dances.

Parents talking

❝ We took our son's school reading book on holiday with us. On our way to the beach we visited a local zoo. My son dropped the book over a ledge. We felt real fools when we got back home, trying to explain to the headmaster that his book was lying at the bottom of a snake pit in Ibiza! ❞

Useful books for five- to six-year-olds

English

(Collections of stories)

Selected Fairy Tales, Barbara Leonie Picard (ed.) (OUP)
Sing a Song of Sixpence, Vince Cross and Nick Sharratt (ed.) (OUP)
The Kingfisher Treasury of Nursery Stories, Susan Price (ed.) (Kingfisher)
The Worm and the Toffee-nosed Princess and other stories, Eva Ibbotson (Pan Macmillan)
Link-up series, Jessie Reid and Joan Low (ed.) (Collins)
Old Bear Stories, Jane Hissey (Hutchinson)

(Spelling)

The Freezing Alphabet, Posy Simmonds (Cape)
My Picture Dictionary, comp. Betty Matthews (Schofield and Sims)
My First Oxford Dictionary, comp. Evelyn Goldsmith (OUP)
Early Spelling Workbooks, Anne Forster and Paul Martin (Schofield and Sims)

Mathematics

The Number Books, Andrew Parker and Jane Stamford (Schofield and Sims)
Heinemann Maths Games, Margo Fourman, Jo Pilling and Lynda Cockcroft (Heinemann)
Numberland, Suzanne Edwards and Cherrie Wild (Collins)
Simple Maths, Rose Griffiths (A and C Black)

Science

Sarah Scrap and Her Nature Trail, Wendy Lewis (Evans)
Sarah Scrap and Her Wonderful Heap, Wendy Lewis (Evans)
At the Beach, Ann and Harlow Rockwell (Evans)

What Happens When ... (you run, sleep, etc.) Jay Richardson (Evans)
The First Encyclopaedia of Animals, Michael Chinery (Kingfisher)

Design and Technology

Look! First Technology, Cyril Gilbert (Longman)
Things to Make for 5-Year-Olds, Donna Bryant (Pan Macmillan)
Things to Make for 6-Year-Olds, Donna Bryant (Pan Macmillan)

History

A Sense of History series, Sallie Purkis and James Mason (Longman)
How Children Lived, Chris and Melanie Rice (Dorling Kindersley)

Geography

Mapstart 1, Simon Catling (Collins)
First Geography Workbooks, Susan Thomas (OUP)

Art

First Faces, Snazaroo (Kingfisher)
Five Minute Faces, Snazaroo (Kingfisher)
Fantastic Faces, Snazaroo (Kingfisher)

Music

Listening to Music, (book and cassette) Helen MacGregor (Longman)

CHAPTER THREE

Year 2 – Ages six to seven

❝ She won't tell me a thing about what she gets up to at school. It might as well be a private club or a secret society for all I get to hear about it! ❞

Year 2 is the final year your child will spend in the infant school. It will be a very busy time for her, because this is where the pressure begins to increase, even in the happiest and best-run of schools. It is often also a time when she begins to talk less at home about her school life.

If this happens do not let it bother you. Your child is beginning to develop and this means that she wants to have more things that she can call her own. School is one of these personal possessions. If she starts to become incommunicative it does not mean that she is drawing away from you; she is becoming a person in her own right. She is also becoming very busy. Not only is her teacher revising all the things that were taught in Year 1, but she is also introducing her to many new facts and skills. This is partly because between the ages of six and seven, children often begin to spurt ahead in their capacity and willingness to learn. It is also because during this year your child and all the others in her class will be taking the National Assessment Tests.

YEAR 2 – AGES SIX TO SEVEN

Teachers are human. They want the children in their charge to do well and will be striving to bring them to a pitch where they will do justice to themselves. After the tests, of course, they are just as busy filling in any gaps the results of the tests have revealed in the children's skills and knowledge. These tests are dealt with in the next chapter. In the meantime there is still plenty that you can do to reinforce the National Curriculum activities. Even if your child may be clamming up about what she is doing at school, she will still want your love and attention at home and will appreciate taking part in activities with you.

National Curriculum in English

Children will be expected to:

- talk and listen with confidence in a number of different situations, showing an increasing grasp of standard English and showing in their responses that they understand the main points of what they have been told;
- read independently with increasing understanding across a wider range of material;
- produce writing which is organised, imaginative and clear.

Reading, speaking and listening

Collaborate with the school and try to turn your child into a fluent reader as quickly as possible. She will make very little progress in any of the National Curriculum subjects until she can read well.

By this age your child will be moving on from fairy tales and myths to more contemporary forms of writing. While she will still enjoy reading tales of magic and fantasy she will also want to read more about children of her own age, with similar backgrounds and problems. These stories, of course, will have to be written in simple language and use concepts that she can understand.

A number of publishing houses issue whole series of such books aimed at six- to seven-year-olds and these are stocked by most libraries and large bookshops. These books are usually between 2000 and 4000 words long, well illustrated, up to date, written by experts in the field, and recommended to arouse and hold the interest of most young children with a limited concentration span.

Provide your child with a steady supply of these books over the year. Read some of them together and let her read others on her own or with brothers and sisters, grandparents, etc.

Using current events

Take every opportunity to utilise the interest which may be aroused by something that is happening around you. If everyone in the family is excited about a holiday, such as Easter or Christmas, try to provide stories about these events for your child to read and identify with.

Read the messages and inscriptions on Christmas and birthday cards. If you are going away somewhere, try to find simple brochures and booklets about the place for her to study and read. If she is being taken to a football match or a pantomime or play, try to find or borrow old programmes. The language may be too difficult, but there will be pictures to study and it will reinforce the conviction that reading is an essential part of life.

A bonfire night English project

Shortly before bonfire night ask your child to read the poem which starts:

'Please to remember
The fifth of November . . .'

and then:

Learn the poem and say it aloud.

Read the story of the real Guy Fawkes and why he is still remembered.

Make a list of the names of all the fireworks you can remember.

Link with art to draw pictures of fireworks.
Describe and imitate the noises made by different fireworks.
Use musical instruments – drums, etc. – to help you make
these sounds.
Write down a list of instructions on how to handle fireworks
safely.
Link with design and technology and plan and make your
own guy.
Try to write your own short poem about bonfire night.
Talk about the care of pets and other animals on bonfire
night. Write down a list of things to do to help them.

Here are some other occasions which could be used as springboards for written work: Christmas, Diwali, Shrove Tuesday,
Thanksgiving, St George's Day.

Predicting and changing endings

At this age your child is getting more and more independent and
wanting to think for herself and beginning to make her own decisions. Utilise this desire by giving her chances to think and talk
about the books she is reading.

When your child is half-way through a book see if she can predict the end. What will happen to the leading characters? Will
they achieve what they want? How will they do this? Talk about
the ending and write a few notes saying what your child thinks
will happen.

With more familiar stories try a different approach and change
the endings by saying 'What if ...?' 'What if Cinderella had not
gone to the ball?' 'What if the woodman had not rescued Little
Red Riding Hood?'

The Sleeping Beauty

Read the story of *The Sleeping Beauty*.
What might have happened in the story if the following

changes had taken place:

- All the fairies at the Christening party disliked the baby, so each one put a different curse on her.
- The princess became very tough and overcame all the curses and grew up to be happy.
- The princess did not prick her finger and instead of falling asleep she decided to modernise the palace.
- When the handsome prince turned up the princess did not like him.

What other changes could be made?

Think of alternative endings to *Snow White and the Seven Dwarfs, Hansel and Gretel, Jack and the Beanstalk,* etc.

Quizzes

In order to help your child think about what she has read and respond to it appropriately, organise short question and answer quizzes together. These might consist of questions about stories which have been read or more general English language quizzes. For example: opposites (big – small etc.); words with similar meanings (loud – noisy, etc.); sounds made by animals (lion – roars, etc.); homes of animals (dog – kennel, etc.); male and female (boy – girl, etc.); or parents and young (sheep – lamb, etc.). Encourage your child to answer quickly and concisely. See if she can make up some questions about a book you have both read, and test you with them.

Collecting examples

Emphasise the fact that there are many different forms of reading and writing by starting to collect and discuss examples of these. In addition to books, help your child to make a collection of labels, instructions, leaflets, programmes, announcements, headlines, song lyrics, slogans, etc. Go through them together, read them aloud and decide what the intention of each different piece of writing is. Encourage your child to try to copy some of these different forms.

Writing

The teacher will continue to encourage her children to write in a variety of styles and for a variety of readers. She will divide these forms of writing into two main sorts:

- chronological writing, or stories and accounts,
- non-chronological writing – lists, labels, etc.

She will attempt to be as ingenious as possible in the projects she sets the children, because if the children do not enjoy writing they will not try very hard at it, and will not do it well.

Do your best to help your child understand and enjoy the purposes of writing. Show her, by your own example, that some forms of writing are a pleasure and that others are very useful. You will be doing her a great service at this age if you can encourage her to organise and present writing in different ways and to write with confidence and accuracy. One or two fifteen-minute slots a week should still be sufficient to keep your child interested, develop her confidence and polish some of the skills described below.

Titles

Talk together about your favourite books and their titles. What is the point of a title of a story? It should tell us something about the contents of the book and be interesting enough to make us want to read the book. Get your child to think of alternative suitable titles for her favourite stories – *Little Red Riding Hood, Jack and the Beanstalk, Cinderella, Puss in Boots, Dick Whittington*, etc. She could then select one of these alternative titles and design the front cover of the book, using her new title and a suitable illustration. Talk about a character in a book, for example, Snow White. What do you think she looked like? What sort of person was she? Would you have done the things that she did? How did she treat the seven dwarfs? What does this tell us about her?

Point of view

Encourage your child to rewrite one of her favourite stories as it might gave been told by one of the other characters in it. Write *Snow White and the Seven Dwarfs* as it might have been written by one of the dwarfs. How would the story of *The Three Little Pigs* go if it was written by the wolf?

The 7-League Boots

What would you do if you found the magic boots used in the story? Would you use them to become a good runner or footballer?

Write the story as if it had been written by the ogre.

What do you think would be another good title for the story?

Draw around the edges of a shoe on a piece of cardboard, so that you have the shape of a shoe. Inside the shape write down all the words you can think of to do with feet and shoes.

Writing across the curriculum

In Year 2 the teacher will be using your child's increasing grasp of English to ask her to undertake writing activities in most of the other subjects of the curriculum – history, geography, and so on. This is known as *writing across the curriculum*. It is intended to show the child the importance of writing in all aspects of life and in all the subjects she will be learning at school.

Often the teacher will base this writing across the curriculum on a book or story. Using the book as a springboard she will take different aspects of it to interest the child in history, geography, etc. This is a very useful project to embark upon at home. It will help your child to understand that she can use her newly acquired writing skills in all the other subjects of the National Curriculum. Most reading books, stories and poems may be divided up into sections for different types of follow-up writing. If your child is really interested in one particular book, a story or an account of dinosaurs, or whatever, use this enthusiasm as the basis for all sorts of writing. The following example shows how a story can be used across the curriculum.

Using the *Selfish Giant* for writing activities
The outline of the story is that a selfish giant bans children from his lovely garden. As a result the garden shrivels up and dies. The remorseful giant allows the children back in and the garden blooms again, but the giant dies.

English   Write the story from the point of view of one of the children. Make a list of the flowers and plants which could have been in the garden. Compose a notice written by the giant to keep the children out.

Art   Draw a picture of the giant's garden in bloom. Underneath the picture label the plants and flowers in the garden.

Science   Explain how the giant would have planted and looked after his plants. What natural reasons could cause the garden to wither and die?

History   Compare modern garden tools with pictures of tools used in the past.

Geography   What weather conditions are needed for gardens to grow? Why do gardens not grow in some parts of the world?

Technology   Make a magnifying glass to look at minibeasts in the garden. Twist a paper clip into a loop. Place the loop in water. Look through the water stretched across the loop. It will magnify objects. Explain what *magnify* means.

Maths   Count and record the different colours of flowers in your garden or the local park.

Alphabetical order

By this time most children should know the letters of the alphabet by heart, or at least be able to recognise the letters when they see them written down. They should be given practice in using the basic principles of alphabetical order because this is one of the important tools for the use of English.

Practising alphabetical order

Write down a few letters of the alphabet out of order. Ask your child to rewrite them, placing them in the correct order. Start with three or four letters. Gradually increase the number of letters used. Go on to placing simple words in alphabetical order, for example dog   apple   crash.

The mechanics of writing

The teacher will try to ensure that her children:

- are using sentences with full stops and capital letters;
- write sensible sentences;
- begin to use questions and question marks;
- get plenty of practice in spelling words of one and two syllables;
- begin to join the letters they use together into a simple form of joined writing.

You can help at home by letting your child write fluently and with enthusiasm, but afterwards going through what she has written with her and pointing out common mistakes. Do not expect too much in the way of correct grammar at this age. Concentrate on helping her to write short sentences containing capital letters and full stops. By this stage she should also be able to spell many short words containing only one syllable.

Handwriting

Find out if the school will be starting joined writing this year, and what form it will take. Most schools start this in the last year of the infants, as the National Curriculum suggests, but others wait until the first junior year. If the school is going to teach it in Year 2 give your child practice in joining letters together with loops. Begin to copy short poems and other pieces of writing, taking care to make letters the same size.

Practising letters

Begin writing sentences with a large number of given letters in them – a b c and so on, to practise forming the letters in the same way, making them the same size:

a: The actor ate all the apples in the abbey.
b: Boys brought bubbles to the babbling brook.

Grammar

A great deal of education, especially at this age, consists of simple repetition. Throughout the year concentrate on helping your child to understand and practise the basic aspects of sentence construction. If she can grasp these the rest of the English curriculum in the junior school next year will become that much easier for her.

Make sure that your child knows what *letters*, *words* and *sentences* are. Encourage her to make up her own sentences, drawing upon her vocabulary. Check that she is using capital letters and full stops in the right places. Read sentences in books together, pointing out the capital letters and full stops. Practise putting question marks at the end of suitable sentences. Give your child practice in writing lines of question marks, explaining that we put one at the end of a sentence which asks a question.

Jumbled sentences

Give your child practice in sorting out jumbled sentences and putting the words in the right order, using capital letters and full stops as appropriate, for example:
book bring the me – Bring me the book.
is where he – Where is he?

Spelling

There is a great debate in infant schools as to whether spelling is 'caught' or 'taught', that is does a child learn to spell by wide reading, thus assimilating almost unconsciously how to spell words, or should there be a definite effort to teach children how to spell words. As with most educational questions, the answer is a little of both. The more your child reads the more accustomed she will become to the sight of words and the easier she will find it to spell them. However, the process will be speeded up if she is taught to look for patterns in the spelling of words, and you can definitely help her here.

Start to keep a personal dictionary in a notebook at home. As the child comes across a new word which she asks you to explain or spell for her, enter it in the notebook. This should help her understand how important writing things down can be. It will also help her to get used to the idea of referring to books to find or check information, which will become one of the most important aspects of the National Curriculum at Key Stage 2.

Patterns of spelling

Collect and learn words containing the same sounds:
ung: flung, jungle, bung, rung, dung, etc.
ain: rain, brain, drain, main, etc.
ack: back, crack, jack, smack, rack, etc.
ock: rock, sock, dock, lock, etc.

Vowels

Revise the vowels: a e i o u
Give your child a number of incomplete words and ask her to
complete them by inserting a vowel in each gap:
b....ck d....g f....sh p....t

Problems

❝ *My daughter has started writing all right, but it all
seems so shapeless! She goes on for page after page
with her stories, with hardly any punctuation. Surely
there should be a bit more form and discipline to
her writing by now?* ❞

This is a common problem, but there is no real need to worry.
Far from it. Your daughter has made a breakthrough. She has
discovered that she can put down her thoughts and feelings in
writing and this is very good. She is rambling on because she
is a bit drunk with the power of it all. It is a bit like learning to
ride a bicycle and then spending all the hours of daylight on it.
Don't try to dissuade your daughter yet and make her slow
down. A lot of work in the top infants is messy like this. Just be
pleased that she has taken to writing. It can be shaped and
ordered in the junior school. The great American novelist
Ernest Hemingway once said 'If you do it first you can't do it
pretty!' He meant that if you are pioneering a new writing style, as
he was, then the creative aspect is going to be so important that
the actual writing might become a bit rough at the edges at times.
This is what is happening with your daughter. She has discovered
a new power. Encourage it and let her get on with it for the time
being.

National Curriculum mathematics

During this year the teacher will:

- revise and consolidate the work done in Year 1 and before that in the reception class;
- encourage the children to try different ways of approaching problems and finding answers;
- teach children to recognise and understand increasingly difficult numbers;
- use the 2, 5 and 10 multiplication tables;
- go on to more advanced ways of measuring shapes;
- begin to use simple tables and diagrams.

You can help your daughter at home by developing the practical use of mathematics, showing her the importance of understanding basic facts and concepts in order to be able to use them in everyday life. She will not be able to understand the theoretical parts of mathematics she will soon be encountering in the National Curriculum unless she masters the practical aspects at this early age.

Number

Make sure that your child can recognise numbers, first up to 500 and then to 1000. Help her to count in tens – 10 20 30 40; 18 28 38 48 etc.

Work with her to help her understand the concept that there are different ways of making a number, for example, 20 can be made up of 15 + 5, 10 + 10, 14 + 6, etc.

Use combinations of counters to help your child learn the two times and five times tables. Practise simple adding up and taking away with single figures (3 + 4), then double figures (10 + 12).

Use numbers in simple problems: 'If a child has four pencils, loses one and finds three more, how many will he end up with?' Go shopping and involve the addition and subtraction of money and make and use shopping lists.

At this stage your child will be taking away tens and units, and later hundreds, tens and units. This process will often involve 'carrying over' figures from the units to the tens, and from the tens to the hundreds. There are two ways of doing this: *decomposition* and *equal addition*. Find out from your child's teacher which method she is teaching before you help at home.

Decomposition

With decomposition, a ten is borrowed from the top line of the tens column and added to the top line of the units column:

$$_2\cancel{3}^{1}2$$
$$1\ 8-$$
$$\overline{1\ 4}$$

Equal addition

With equal addition, a ten is added to the bottom line of the tens and the top line of the units:

$$3^{1}2$$
$$_2\cancel{1}\ 8-$$
$$\overline{1\ 4}$$

Calculator activities

Revise last year's activities. Say that you will call out a number, but when you do so you want your child to enter a number four higher than the one called out.

See how many ways you can make ten in the window.

Begin to check answers to addition and subtraction sums.

Count in twos and fours on the calculator.

Roll a die and enter the number into the calculator.

Measuring

Embark upon simple measuring activities. Start with non-standard measurements to help your child understand the basic principles of judging and recording sizes and weights. This means measuring using everyday things, instead of rulers, scales, etc. Measure objects using the span of your child's hand, the size of her foot, the length of her thumb, and so on. Estimate or guess the number of jugs of water it will take to fill a bowl, and then check. See if you can find something which will weigh approximately as much as another object.

Time

Help your child to grow accustomed to the concept of time by looking at the calendar every day and noting the date. On the calendar mark your child's birthday and those of friends and relations. Look at the date on newspapers. Begin to practise counting in fives, to accustom children to five-minute intervals on a clock-face. Talk about things which move *slowly* and *quickly*. How many times can your child throw a beanbag in the air and catch it while you time her for one minute? Begin to tell the time by working with a model clock-face with moveable hands. To begin with start with the hours – 4 o'clock, 8 o'clock, and then the half hours – half-past 6, half-past 10.

Shape, space and measures

Help your child to understand ways in which shapes are important in our lives and how they may be measured, by working with her on a number of practical activities.

Fold pieces of paper into halves and quarters, using these terms, and colour them in. Use coloured sticky paper to make triangles, squares and rectangles of different sizes, using the correct terms as you cut them out together. Make collections of patterns in nature – flowers, leaves, etc. Make a study of the shapes and designs of everyday things. Why are torches, toothbrushes and mugs the shapes and sizes that they are?

Begin to look at *symmetry*, study objects which are exactly the same on either side of an imaginary line drawn down the middle. Look for examples of symmetry around the house. Use pieces of fabric or paper to represent one half of a symmetrical shape – a cross, square, etc. Ask your child to use the same material and complete the shape, making sure that it is symmetrical.

3-D shapes
Work on the differences between 2-D (two-dimensional, or flat) and 3-D (three-dimensional, or having depth) shapes.
Examine (2-D) pictures of triangles and (3-D) models of triangles. This should help your child to appreciate that the diagrams in books have their counterparts in real life. Examine a number of 3-D shapes and then discuss them, comparing types of surface, number of sides, number of corners, etc.

National Curriculum science

In Year 2 the teacher will be helping children to:

- think and act in a scientific manner;
- plan experimental work;
- obtain and consider evidence.

She will be carrying out these activities in three main areas of science:

- life processes and living things (animals and plants);
- materials and their properties (rocks, wood, metal, etc.);
- physical processes (force, movement, electricity, etc.).

Help your child to think in a scientific manner and to investigate by observing, measuring, testing and predicting what ought to happen in given circumstances, and recording what she has done.

Life processes and living things

Help your child to develop her understanding of living and non-living things and the differences between them.

Growing things

In order for plants to grow, they need air, sunlight and water, plus a source of minerals. Over the course of a year help your child to carry out and record experiments on growth. Carry out *control* experiments with the same sort of plants. Grow one group exposed to sunlight, air and water, but deprive other groups of one of these necessities and discuss and write about what happens. The plants exposed to sunlight, air and water should grow normally, while the others should not do nearly as well.

Observing animals

Help your child to see how animals grow by keeping some of them. Collect water plants from a pond and place them in a jar with water and mud from the source. Place water beetles from the same place in the jar and describe what happens.

Fill a tin with earth. Put some worms in the tin and place a lid with air-holes over it. Leave the tin in a dark place for a week. Then open the tin and look inside. What have the worms done to the soil?

Don't forget to release the minibeasts back into their natural habitat and to stress to your child the importance of handling the creatures with care.

Materials and their properties

Help your child to recognise the similarities and differences between materials, to discover the uses of materials and the fact that some materials can be changed by heating or cooling. Show your child that people choose materials for specific purposes in everyday life.

YEAR 2 – AGES SIX TO SEVEN

Examining materials

Collect and examine different kinds of materials and decide why they are used for particular purposes. For example, why are some toys made of metal and others, like floppy dolls, of soft fabrics?

Collect scraps of carpet and draw the patterns, using the colours of each piece. Compare textures and patterns. Try to think of simple, safe tests for testing the strength, damp-resistance etc. of the different pieces. Repeat this with scraps of wallpaper, plastic or tiles.

Testing strength

Collect a number of yoghurt pots, each of the same size and shape. Suspend each one from a series of hooks in the wall using different materials such as string, thread, wire, etc. Now fill each pot with heavy weights. Do any of the materials holding the pot break? Which material seems the weakest?

Project on buildings

Look at different buildings in the area.
What materials are they made of?
Why are different parts of buildings made of different materials – stone, wood, glass, etc.?

Physical processes

Look at different types of *force* – pushing, pulling, dragging, rolling, etc. – in an effort to understand that forces can make things speed up, slow down or change direction. Examine examples of light and sound in action, and revise the fact that many everyday appliances use electricity. Observing all possible safety precautions, show your child how to link a battery by copper wires to a small bulb to construct an electrical circuit and light the bulb. Look at how a torch works and try to see what happens when it is turned on and off.

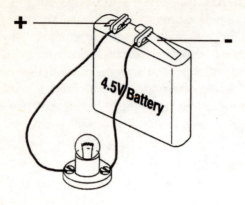

Forces

Experiment with different ways of moving a piece of wood across a flat surface – pushing it, pulling it, placing it on rollers etc. Predict which way you think will be the best. Use different magnets to draw the same number of filings across a table. Which magnets attract the filings from the greatest distance?

Problems

> ❝ *Isn't it dangerous to try to help my child with subjects like science when I don't know anything about them?* ❞

This is a bit like the man feeling uneasy when he was told that he had been procrastinating, because he didn't know what the word meant. Science is all around us, especially at this stage. With infants you do not have to mess about with bunsen burners and retorts. A pleasant walk in the park, looking at growing and moving things and seeing what is changing and what is remaining the same, will provide more than enough science for six- and seven-year-olds.

National Curriculum design and technology

The teacher will:

- revise the previous year's activities;
- help children to select tools, plan events, design objects and then make and test them;
- pay proper regard to safety.

You can help at home by encouraging your child to embark upon simple 'making' activities, using different tools and materials.

A papier-mâché head

A papier-mâché construction will involve your child in all aspects of the design and technology curriculum. Involve your child in making a person's head. Work out what the head will represent – a policeman, a pirate, a cook, etc., and then design the head on paper.

Go through the technique of making a papier-mâché head with your child. Blow up a balloon and tape a large, flat piece of paper around it for the base. Now tear up newspaper into small pieces and soak the pieces in paste. Stick five or six layers of torn up newspaper over the balloon and its paper base.

When the papier-mâché has dried completely, deflate the balloon with a pin. You are now ready to paint the head an appropriate colour and attach hair and features, using sections of egg-boxes, raffia, etc. Finish off the features, using paint or felt-tip. If your child seems particularly adept at this sort of work give her an extra problem. Ask her to make the head leaving a hole at the base through which a stick could be placed to make the head move, like that of a puppet.

National Curriculum history

This year the teacher will probably be concentrating on such projects as:

- homes, roads and transport and similar everyday objects, showing how they have evolved and changed over the centuries;

- stories of people and events in history.

Over this year you can best help your child by letting her read and listen to famous stories from the past, and developing a sense of the difference between *now* and *then*. Look at pictures in books and talk about the ways in which people lived and dressed at different times. The following well-known characters from history will provide plenty to talk about: *Horatius at the bridge*; *Building the Pyramids*; *Hannibal and the elephants*; *The wooden horse of Troy*; *Joseph and his coat*; *Dick Turpin's ride*; *Guy Fawkes*; *The children's crusade.*

National Curriculum geography

Over the course of this year the teacher will:

- look at two different localities with her children – one of these will be the area around the school, and the other will either be another area in the United Kingdom, or a locality overseas;
- continue to study the environment, comparing areas and physical features;
- introduce children to basic geographical terms like *river, mountain, hill*, etc.;
- undertake activities connected with the weather.

An important aspect of geography which can be studied at home in this year is that of map-making. Combine this with a study of your neighbourhood and your child will learn to think in geographical terms which will help her with her curriculum work at school. Let your child study your house and make maps of it, showing the location of the different rooms and the siting of the main items of furniture in the rooms. From this she could go on to make an illustrated study of the houses close by. In your company she could make sketches and draw maps, at the same time learning the basic vocabulary of homes – *detached, semi-detached, terraced, bungalows, flats*, etc.

What facilities are there outside the houses – street lighting, pedestrian crossings, etc.? What conditions are the roads and pavements in? Compare her drawings with pictures of homes in other countries.

Help your child to make a study of shops in the neighbourhood. How many are there? What do they sell? How are the goods weighed, measured and wrapped? How are the shops kept clean and tidy? Draw maps showing the location of the different stores.

National Curriculum art

The teacher will continue to explore two areas of art:

- investigating and making;
- knowledge and understanding.

On the practical side she will:

- revise the previous year's activities;
- continue to encourage her children to record their ideas and findings;
- work practically and imaginatively with tools, materials and techniques they have selected for their effectiveness;
- continue to help the children use the knowledge of art which they are accumulating in practical ways in their own work.

At home, you can work with your child on different art activities, so that she can practise and develop the skills which she is learning at school.

Mosaics

Show your child pictures of mosaics, or visit a museum which has some. Explain that they were made by Romans, Greeks and other people in the past. Ask her to make her own simple mosaic out of buttons. Begin by drawing a simple outline picture on cardboard or wood, and then stick the buttons over the picture. Look for other materials with which to make mosaics, such as rice or pasta.

Montage

Make a montage of features on paper. Cut out features from photographs in newspapers and magazines – ears, noses, mouths, etc. – and glue them on to paper making fresh faces, matching eyes from one photograph with a nose from another and a mouth from a third, and so on. Make similar montages out of pictures of different parts of motor cars, ships, plants, etc.

2-D and 3-D

Reinforce the difference between 2-D and 3-D shapes by adding 3-D shapes to 2-D drawings and paintings. Draw and paint a motor car, without wheels. Stick small tin-lids on to the painting to represent wheels. Paint the wheels to match the car. Do the same thing by sticking a 3-D shield on to a drawing of a roman soldier. Look for other ways of matching 2-D and 3-D artwork.

National Curriculum music

The teacher will continue to give her children opportunities to:

- listen to and assess music;
- perform and compose their own forms of music.

Let your child see you listening to and enjoying music at home. Help her to develop a sense of rhythm by listening to recordings of simple songs and then discussing them, working out different rhythms. Ask her to clap in time to the music and then to beat a simple percussion instrument in time to it, or beat on a table top. Let her clap in time to a number of different clocks. See if she can simulate the beating of a clock by using a 'beater' on a surface.

National Curriculum physical education

Throughout this year the teacher will continue to concentrate on activities involving:

- games;
- gymnastics;
- dance.

She will attempt to give the children confidence in their bodies and the ability to work as members of a team.

You can do your part by continuing to play games with your child and encouraging her to run, jump, throw, catch, etc. Stress the importance of playing fairly and being a good loser.

Gymnastics

By the end of the infant stage most children will be expected to perform simple gymnastic activities, so any help you can provide in encouraging your child to perform forward rolls, cartwheels and headstands will be of great use. Try to persuade her to display her increasing control by performing *sequences* of movements – headstand into forward roll into cartwheel, and so on. Introduce the concept of *direction*, by asking your child to face different directions at various parts of the sequences.

Balance

Ask your child to move and stop, using different balances. She should travel using any type of movement – walking, running, hopping, etc. and on command, stop, and balance on any part of her body – feet, seat, knees, etc. On command she should move on, using a different type of movement, and on command, stop again, this time using another part of the body. Carry on in this fashion.

Dance

Ask your child to perform different mimes, both with and without taped music, for example, snakes crawling, rabbits playing, etc. Go on to moving in response to different taped stimuli – music, drum beats, clapping, etc.

A toy dance

Devise and perform a dance to the theme of 'toys'.
Select some suitable music to accompany your child, and talk

about what toys you would find in a toyshop.
Imagine that one by one these toys come to life and start dancing.
Select and perform suitable movements for each toy.
Go on to dance like puppets on a string.

Games

Encourage your child to move freely and to observe rules by playing various chasing games with her – tag, etc. Give your child different pieces of apparatus, such as hoops and beanbags, and see if she can make up simple games with objectives and rules. Play dodging games in which your child has to avoid small balls and beanbags which you throw gently at her. Work in advance with your child to make up objectives and rules for these games.

Devise and play games involving hoops. Bowl a hoop and chase it and then set off in a different direction when you have caught it. Repeat the game but use the other hand to bowl the hoop. Spin several hoops and move from one to the other, keeping them all spinning. Skip with a hoop, setting a target of skips.

End of Year 2 checklists

Most, but not all children should be able to meet the majority of these targets by the end of Year 2. They should also, of course, still be able to meet the requirements set for the end of Year 1 given at the end of Chapter 2.

English

Speaking and listening
The child:

- can use the right words and phrases to explain something;
- can listen and reply showing that she understands what is being talked about;

- can understand how talking has to be shaped to meet its listeners;
- can participate in drama and improvisations.

Reading
The child:

- can read with fluency and enjoyment;
- can talk about, predict the outcome of and retell stories;
- can use and organise reference materials.

Writing
The child:

- can understand and enjoy the purposes of writing;
- can organise and present writing in different ways;
- can write with confidence and accuracy;
- can plan her writing and rewrite when necessary.

Grammar
The child is developing a knowledge of grammar and simple punctuation, especially sentences, full stops, capital letters and question marks.

Handwriting
The child is developing a legible form of handwriting, forming letters with care.

Spelling
The child is beginning to spell simple words with increasing confidence.

Mathematics

Number
The child:

- can recognise numbers up to 50;
- can count in twos and fours;

- can measure using non-standard units;
- can tell the time;
- is beginning to understand thousands, hundreds, tens and units;
- can operate a calculator;
- can add and subtract hundreds, tens and units;
- can record in a number of ways.

Shape, space and measures
The child:

- can recognise halves and quarters of shapes;
- can understand why manufactured objects are the shape they are;
- can recognise angles.

Science

Life processes and living things
The child:

- understands the differences between living things and things which have never lived;
- understands how animals live, feed, grow and use their senses;
- knows the external parts of the human body and why humans need to eat and drink, exercise, excrete and reproduce;
- knows the external part of plants and how they grow and reproduce;
- understands that living things can be grouped according to similarities and differences;
- is beginning to study and learn about the environment.

Materials and their properties
The child:

- can group and sort materials;
- can recognise common materials and their uses;

- knows that some materials can change shape when force is exerted;
- knows that some materials change when they are heated or cooled.

Physical processes

The child:

- has worked with simple electrical circuits;
- understands about different types of force and movement;
- understands that there are different sources of light and sound.

Design and technology

Designing skills

The child:

- can use his experience and can discuss with others to produce plans;
- can shape, assemble and rearrange objects during the planning process;
- can use drawings and models to develop ideas;
- can identify the strengths and weaknesses of ideas.

Making skills

The child:

- can select materials, tools and techniques;
- can measure, mark out, cut and shape;
- can assemble, join and finish products;
- can make suggestions about how to proceed;
- can test and evaluate what he has made.

History

The child:

- is developing an awareness of the past;
- is beginning to understand that things happened chronologically, e.g. that the Stone Age came before the Romans;

- understands some of the ways we find out about the past – books, pictures, etc.;
- can use the present as a starting point to study the past;
- is beginning to learn about famous lives;
- is beginning to learn about past events.

Geography

The child:

- is investigating her environment;
- is developing skills and knowledge to help her investigations;
- is studying broader aspects of the world and one other locality;
- is learning simple geographical terms;
- is learning about the effects of the weather;
- understands about the uses of land and buildings.

Art

Investigating and making
The child:

- can record ideas and feelings;
- can represent what she has seen and touched;
- can choose resources and materials;
- can use tools, materials and techniques;
- can present work in two and three dimensions.

Knowledge and understanding
The child:

- can describe and compare works of art;
- can use knowledge gained to help her own work.

Music

Performing and composing
The child:

- can use sounds and respond to music;

- can sing songs and play pieces;
- can improvise musical patterns;
- can record musical compositions.

Listening and appraising
The child:

- can recognise how sounds can be made in different ways;
- can recognise how sounds are used to achieve different effects in music;
- can recognise that music comes from different times and places;
- can respond to music with dance and other forms of expression;
- can describe sounds heard and performed.

Physical education

Games
The child:

- can play simple competitive games;
- can use balls and other equipment;
- can move using space and is aware of others.

Gymnastics
The child:

- can move in different ways;
- can link movements into sequences;
- can repeat these movements and sequences.

Dance
The child:

- can control her coordination and balance;
- can perform movements gracefully;
- can explore feelings and moods and respond appropriately to music.

Parents talking

> I used to get really uptight when my son started writing about his favourite people in our English sessions at home. He wrote about footballers and pop stars and television comedians. All the time I was thinking, "What about me? I'm your mother. I should be in there somewhere!"

> His father and I helped Peter at home with his project on comparing materials. It was fascinating, at least I thought so. Then I looked up from comparing the weights of three different objects and found that I had been talking to myself for the last half hour. Peter and his father were out in the garden playing football.

Useful books for six- to seven-year-olds

English (Reading books)

The Teddybears series, Sussana Gretz and Alison Sage (A and C Black)

Fables of La Fontaine, adapted by Brian Wildsmith (OUP)

The Tim Books series, Edward Ardizzone (OUP)

The Faber Book of Golden Fairytales, Sara and Stephen Corrin (eds) (Faber)

Max the Cat series, Terrance Dicks (Young Corgi)

Mathematics

Take Off series (*Numbers, Measuring, Time*, etc.), Nancy Hewitt (Evans)

Posters (*Shapes, Numbers*) (Schofield and Sims)

YEAR 2 – AGES SIX TO SEVEN

Science

Earth Calendar, Una Jacobs (A and C Black)
Flower Calendar, Una Jacobs (A and C Black)
Fun with Simple Science, Barbara Taylor (Kingfisher)

Design and Technology

Would you Believe It...? series (*Shells, Stones,* etc.), Catherine Chambers (Evans)
Primary Technology Key Stage 1 series (*London Bridge,* etc.), Eileen Chadwick (Collins)

History

Oxford Primary History Key Stage 1 series (*The Vikings, Christopher Columbus,* etc.), Valerie Fawcett, Pat Hughes and Tim Vicary (OUP)
History Mysteries series (*At School, Cooking,* etc.), Gill Tanner and Tim Wood (A and C Black)

Geography

Young Discoverers series (*Maps and Mapping, Rivers and Oceans,* etc.), Barbara Taylor and David Glover (Kingfisher)

Music

Tinder-Box – 66 Songs for Children, Sylvia Barratt and Sheena Hodge (A and C Black)

Art

Famous Faces, Norman Messenger (Dorling Kindersley)

CHAPTER FOUR

Key Stage 1 Assessment Tests

> ❛ *We get messages from school saying that these tests are no big thing and that the children should be allowed to take them in their stride. Then if you go into the school just before the tests the teachers are rushing about like headless chickens. The kids may be laid-back about the tests, but the teachers certainly aren't, and neither are most parents!* ❜

When your child is about seven she will take tests in English, mathematics and science. These tests will be set between March and May of her final year in the infants. This is the year in which the majority of the children in the class are seven. If your child is slightly younger than the average she may only be six when she takes the tests.

All the tests are graded at different levels from 1 to 10. At the end of Key Stage 1 most children are expected to score between Levels 1 and 3. A typical child should achieve Level 2. Some will go on to higher grades. The standards expected at Level 3 are those shown in the checklists at the end of Chapter 3.

There are different grades of papers for all subjects. Your child's teacher will have a shrewd idea of the standards she is capable of and will enter her for the appropriate papers which will allow her to do herself justice.

Details of the levels reached by·your child in the three Core subjects will be sent to you by the school when they are known. Your child's teacher will also continually be assessing her progress in the other subjects of the curriculum and will let you know what levels she achieves in these, both in writing and verbally at open evenings.

The forms taken by the tests will vary from year to year, but children who have worked easily through the activities of the National Curriculum in Years 1 and 2 should be able to reach Level 2, and some may go on to Level 3 and beyond.

Sample tests

The sample tests given in this chapter are not intended to be exact duplicates of the ones your child will take in Year 2. They do, however, cover the Key Stage 1 curriculum and have been used with many children in the classroom. They should give you some idea of the stage your child has reached.

The tests are designed in a progressive manner, starting with simple activities which should be within the scope of children capable of covering Level 1, and going on to Level 3.

Unfortunately, the size of this book prevents us from reproducing the tests in the same size and format as the 'real thing'. However, if possible, perhaps by getting your child to write down her answers on a separate sheet, let her try all the questions, but do not ask her to spend any time on questions she cannot answer. There is no time limit to the tests given in this chapter. Allow your child to work through them at her own pace. The answers are given at the end of the chapter. If she has difficulty in understanding the meaning of a question you may help her understand what she is supposed to do.

English tests

Children will be tested in their abilities at reading, writing, spelling and handwriting. A typical range of questions is shown below. No handwriting test has been set, but you can monitor your child's progress for yourself here. Judge the handwriting used in the answers to the English questions, especially the stories, looking for neatness, well-shaped letters and letters of the same size.

Spelling

Level 1
1 Spell these words:

e...   d...   b...   f...   j...

p...   c...   b...   z...   b...

b...   s...   c...   h...   b...   m...

p...

f...   t...   f...

KEY STAGE 1 ASSESSMENT TESTS

Level 2

2 Fill in the gaps in the story:

The boy w............t to see his friend who
lived on top of the h............l. They
s............w some bi............s singing on
the branches of some t............s. The boys
went for a w............k but it began to
r............n, so they r............n
h............e again as f............t as they
could.

Level 3

3 These words are not spelt correctly.
Spell them the right way:

    ritch   to have a lot of money

                                        ....

    eegle   a large bird   ....
    aple   a fruit   ....
    frend   someone we like   ....
    nee   part of the leg   ....
    rivver   moving water   ....
    glas   we can see through it

                                          ....

    smal   not big   ....
    appy   to be glad   ....
    shoo   worn on the foot   ....

One mark for each correct answer
Total: 40
Level 1: 1–20
Level 2: 21–30
Level 3: 31–40

Reading

Level 1

Humpty Dumpty

Humpty Dumpty sat on a wall.
Humpty Dumpty had a great fall.
All the king's horses,
And all the king's men
Couldn't put Humpty together again.

1 Who was sitting down? ....
2 What was he sitting on?......................
3 What happened to him?......................
4 Who tried to put him together again?
  (1)...
  (2)...

Going to St Ives

As I was going to St Ives,
I met a man with seven wives,
Every wife had seven sacks,
Every sack had seven cats,
Every cat had seven kits:
Kits, cats, sacks and wives,
How many were there going to St Ives?

5 Where was the writer going? ....
6 Who did he meet on the way?..............
7 What did the man have? ....
8 What was in the sacks? ....
9 What did each cat have?...................
10 What is a *kit*?..................................

KEY STAGE 1 ASSESSMENT TESTS

Level 2

The lion and the unicorn

The lion and the unicorn
Were fighting for the crown;
The lion beat the unicorn
All around the town.

Some gave them white bread,
And some gave them brown;
Some gave them plum cake
And drummed them out of town.

11 Who were fighting?
   (1)..
   (2)..
12 What were they fighting for?...............
13 Who won?......................................
14 Where did the winner beat the loser?

   ....
15 What did people give them?
   (1)..
   (2)..
   (3)..

Level 3

Bobby Shaftoe

Bobby Shaftoe's gone to sea,
Silver buckles at his knee;
He'll come back and marry me,
Bonny Bobby Shaftoe.

Bobby Shaftoe has a hen,
Cockle button, cockle ben,
She lays eggs for gentlemen,
But none for Bobby Shaftoe.

16 Where has Bobby Shaftoe gone............
17 What is he wearing at his knee?..........
18 What will he do when he comes back?
....
19 What bird does he own?.......................
20 Who does she lay eggs for? ....

One mark for each correct answer
Total: 24
Level 1: 1–11
Level 2: 12–20
Level 3: 21–24

Writing

Level 1
1 Make a list of the names of ten
   different fruits. (Marks out of 10)
2 Make a list of ten different animals.
   (Marks out of 10)

Level 2
3 Write down how you would plant seeds
   and look after them until they have
   grown into plants. (Marks out of 10)
4 Write down a sentence about each of
   these: (1 mark for each sentence)

   a school

   a car

   a shop

   a party

   a game

KEY STAGE 1 ASSESSMENT TESTS

Level 3

5 Write a short story called *The House on the Hill*. (Marks out of 15)

Total marks: 50
Level 1: 1–20
Level 2: 21–35
Level 3: 36–50

Mathematics tests

Level 1

1 How many counters are there in each pile?

2 Put a cross over all the shapes which are the same.

3 Put a cross over the smallest thing in each of these groups:

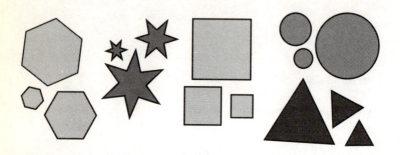

4 What is each of these coins?

5 Fill in these gaps, so that each sum makes 10:

3 + ... = 10
4 + ... = 10
2 + ... = 10
5 + ... = 10
1 + ... = 10

6 Finish off these patterns:

```
1   2   1   2   1   2   ............  ............
3   1   3   1   3   1   ............  ............
4   2   4   2   4   2   ............  ............
1   5   1   5   1   5   ............  ............
2   2   3   2   2   3   ............  ............
```

Level 2

7 Draw a line under the number which is in the *second* place in these lines:

```
1 2 3 4 5 6        8 7 6 5 4 3
                   4 5 6 7 8 9
3 4 5 6 7          9 8 7 6 5 4
```

8 Finish off these sums to show how many coins make 10p:

.... × 2p = 10p
.... × 10p = 10p
.... × 1p = 10p
.... × 5p = 10p

9 Do these adding up sums:

```
8    9    5    3    4    6
 +    +    +    +    +    +
2    1    3    4    3    2
```

10 Do these take away sums:

```
8    4    7    6    9
 -    -    -    -    -
7    3    5    4    8
```

11 What is the time shown on each clock?

12 Put a line under the *odd* numbers in this line:

1 2 3 4 5 6 7 8 9 10

Level 3

13 Put in the missing numbers in this line:

2 4 .... 8 10 14
.... 18 .... 22 ....

14 Do these adding up sums:

12	16	14	15	16
+	+	+	+	+
8	4	3	5	2

15 How many 10s are there in each of these numbers?

50............. 40.............
30............. 20.............
10.............

16   Do these take away sums:

    14 − 6 = ...
    12 − 4 = ...
    16 − 5 = ...
    10 − 4 = ...
    11 − 3 = ...

17   If these counters were divided up into groups, with the same number in each group, how many counters would there be in each group?

18   There are right angles in four of these shapes. Put a cross over the shapes which have right angles.

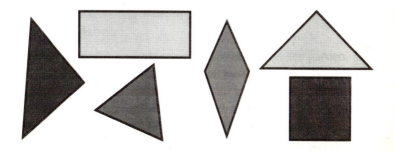

One mark for each correct answer
Total: 85
Level 1: 1–30
Level 2: 31–60
Level 3: 60–85

Science tests

Level 1

1   Put the names of these parts of a plant in the correct box:

flower   root   stem   leaves

2   What three things do plants need to live?

sunl............ a............. wa............

3   Put the names of the parts of the body in the right boxes:

head   neck   arm   chest   waist   leg
hand   foot   knee   ankle   wrist

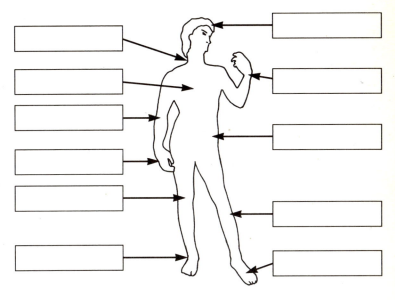

4   What things do people need to stay alive?

f.............   w.............

5   Name five different trees.

Level 2

6   Which animals live in these homes:

nest.................   web....................
hive.................   burrow...............
hole.................

7   Put each of these objects into one of the lines:

badger   bottle   ink   fox   bird
leaf   book   worm   telephone   shoe

Living	*Non-living*

....
....
....
....
....

8 Name three things which would melt in the sun.

....

9 Write **W** under the tree which can be found in the winter.

Write **S** under the tree which can be found in the summer.

10 What sort of weather do you think each of these signs means?

11 These things all give us light. What are they?

Level 3

12 Explain how this electrical circuit works. (Marks out of 5)

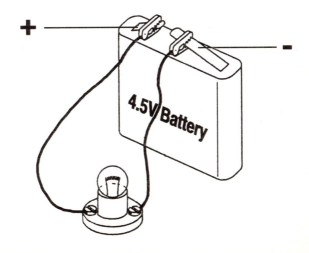

HELP YOUR CHILD THROUGH THE NATIONAL CURRICULUM

13 How could you test these two pillars made out of paper, to say which is the stronger of the two? (Marks out of 5)

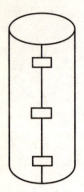
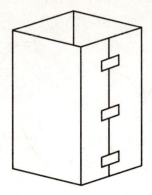

14 This plant is given plenty of water but it has been put into a dark corner of the room. What will happen to it, and why? (Marks out of 5)

One mark for each correct answer
Total: 70
Level 1: 1–25
Level 2: 26–55
Level 3: 56–70

KEY STAGE 1 ASSESSMENT TESTS

Test answers

English – Spelling

1 man, bat, egg, fox, pig, boy, box, cup, jug, peg zip, hen, dog, cat, bell, tree, fly, fire, ball, sea
2 went, hill, saw, birds, trees, walk, rain, ran, home, fast
3 rich, eagle, apple, friend, knee, river, glass, small, happy, shoe

English – Reading

1 Humpty Dumpty, 2 wall, 3 he fell off, 4 the king's horses, the king's men
5 St Ives, 6 a man, 7 seven wives, 8 cats, 9 kits, 10 kitten
11 lion, unicorn, 12 crown, 13 lion, 14 all around the town, 15 white bread, brown bread, plum cake
16 to sea, 17 silver buckles, 18 marry me, 19 hen, 20 gentlemen

English – Writing (words need not be spelt correctly)

1 Give one mark for each fruit.
2 Give one mark for each animal.
3 Select good spot, provide sunlight, air, water.
4 Give a mark for each sentence containing a capital letter, verb and full-stop.
5 Give marks for fluency and a story with a plain beginning, middle and end.

Mathematics

1 3, 5, 2, 7, 8
2 One mark for each triangle with a cross.

3 One mark for each group with smallest object crossed.
4 £1, 2p, 5p, 50p, 10p
5 7, 6, 8, 5, 9
6 1 2, 3 1, 4 2, 1 5, 2 2 3
7 2, 7, 5, 4, 8
8 5, 1, 10, 2
9 10, 10, 8, 7, 7, 8
10 1, 1, 2, 2, 1
11 5 o'clock, 9 o'clock, 2 o'clock, 6 o'clock, 11 o'clock
12 1, 3, 5, 7, 9
13 6, 12, 16, 20, 24
14 20, 20, 17, 20, 18
15 5, 4, 3, 2, 1
16 8, 8, 11, 6, 8
17 5
18 square, rectangle, 2 right-angled triangles

Science

1 flower, root, stem, leaves
2 sunlight, air, water
3 head, neck, arm, chest, waist, leg, hand, foot, knee, ankle, wrist
4 food, water
5 Give credit for any five trees.
6 bird, spider, bee, rabbit, mouse
7 *Living:* badger, fox, bird, leaf, worm; *Non-living:* bottle, ink, book, telephone, shoe
8 Give credit for any three things which would melt, e.g. ice, grease, butter, margarine, etc.
9 *W* beneath tree with no leaves, *S* beneath tree with leaves
10 rain, sun, snow, windy
11 candle, torch, electric light bulb, lantern, sun, match

12 Give credit for saying to connect wires to battery and bulb to allow electricity to flow through circuit.

13 Give credit for suggesting putting increasing amount of weight on top of each pillar until one pillar collapses.

14 It will need sunlight and will die without it.

If your child scores maximum marks on all tests, from Levels 1–3 in a subject, you could let her try the Level 4 tests in Chapter 9 in that subject.

CHAPTER FIVE

Year 3 – Ages seven to eight

> *As a headteacher there are three statements which always strike terror into my heart: "Your school is going to be inspected!" "One of the infants seems to be missing!" and "Mrs Fazakerley is waiting to see you!"*

Year 3 is the first year of the junior section of the primary school. It is a very important year for your child. It is also one of the most difficult age ranges to teach. No sensible headteacher would admit it to the rest of the staff, but this is the class where he wants one of his best teachers. If it can be got right with the seven- to eight-year-olds it will stay with them for the rest of their school lives.

Most children settle well into the junior years, but a few of the less confident sometimes find it difficult at first to make the transition from the warm family atmosphere of a typical infant class to the bustling, more impersonal atmosphere of the junior school, where the pace of life, both in the classroom and the playground, definitely starts to pick up. Some boys and girls find it hard initially to adapt to their new surroundings, especially if they are no longer the oldest and biggest children in the infants, but are now the youngest and smallest recruits to the junior school and have to adjust to a new way of life.

The class teacher will be watching carefully to make sure that each child settles in to the new ambience, but do not be too worried if your child does not adapt immediately to the extra demands being made upon him. If this appears to be the case, almost certainly the class teacher will notice and will contact you to talk about it. However, if she does not do so and your child still appears to be unhappy by half-term, then make an appointment to see the teacher.

The vast majority of children will take eagerly to the new way of life, especially with the help of an understanding teacher and the knowledge that his parents are still taking an interest in his school work and want him to do well at it.

Even if your child seems to want to cut you adrift from the school, do your best to keep in touch with the class teacher. Do it in an informal and friendly manner; none of us wants to be the dreaded Mrs Fazakerley!

Unlike the previous year, when some children will have been reluctant to talk about school, this is the year when they begin to realise that they need all the help they can get! It will not be at all unusual for your child to approach you and say 'I don't understand this work. Will you help me?'

Settling in

If your child seems to be out of his depth in the first few weeks in the junior school there are a number of ways in which you can help him:

- Talk to other parents to see if their children are experiencing any difficulties. It may be a general problem which will resolve itself in time.
- Encourage your child to carry on friendships with other children in the class.
- Organise a small, informal party and invite some of the other children, so that your child continues to regard himself as one of the gang. If he establishes good relationships with his peers it will make the settling in period that much easier.

The Key Stage 2 curriculum

In Year 3 your child has embarked upon the Key Stage 2 level of the National Curriculum. The teacher will first revise all the areas taught at Key Stage 1 and will use the results of the Key Stage 1 Assessment Tests as a guide to the strengths and weaknesses of the children in the class, before going on to plan individual or group work for the children.

Your child will still be studying the same subjects in Year 3, but usually there will be more emphasis on the foundation subjects than there was in the infant school at Key Stage 1. There will be more of a focus on history, geography, design and technology, music, art and physical education. All the same, a considerable amount of time each week will still be devoted to the core subjects of English, mathematics and science.

Collaborating with the school

As usual there are a number of simple facts about your child which you should ascertain from the class teacher at the first open evening of the school.

- What is the attitude of the teacher to parents helping their children at home?
- Are there any specific things she would like you to help with at home?
- Will there be any regular, organised form of homework set and marked by the teacher?
- Which type of subtraction will be used in mathematics – decomposition or equal addition? (See page 61)
- Is there a style sheet showing the form of handwriting to be taught that year?
- Which period of history and which areas in geography will be studied this year?

National Curriculum English

Over this year at school children following the National Curriculum will be expected to build on all they have learnt at Key Stage 1. They will be expected to:

- talk fluently and listen with understanding, exploring, developing and explaining ideas, planning, predicting and investigating, sharing ideas, reading aloud, reporting and describing, talking and listening to a wide range of people, and taking part in a wide variety of drama activities;
- develop as enthusiastic, independent and reflective readers, being introduced to a wide range of suitable literature, and have opportunities to read extensively for their own interest, pleasure and information. They should be encouraged to respond imaginatively to what they have read and learn how to use reference materials effectively;
- write in response to more demanding tasks, beginning to recognise and understand the needs for different types of writing. They should learn to plan, draft and revise different forms of writing. They should begin to use a wider range of punctuation marks, increase their spelling vocabulary and continue to develop a legible form of handwriting.

Helping with reading, speaking and listening

By this age your child will not want to spend as much time with you about the house as he did when he was an infant. Neither will he want to play so many games or take part in as many activities with you. But there is still a great deal of help you can give him, even if it does tend to be of a slightly more formal variety, involving him in more activities on his own, rather than sharing them completely with you.

By this age he should be able to listen to a weekly serial story or watch a developing series on television and be able to recall and talk about the previous week's events. If your child does have a favourite television programme talk to him casually about it and see how much he remembers from week to week, and ask him how he thinks the programme will develop in future episodes.

This is a year in which you can really give your child a great deal of help with reading. At the beginning of the infant stage most children will have had roughly the same limited reading ability. As time passes, however, some children will outstrip others in their ability and willingness to read. By the time they reach the beginning of the junior stage, at age seven, some children will be fluent readers while others will still be struggling with basic texts.

You will have time in your one-to-one relationship with your child to find out which sort of books he enjoys and by encouraging him to read them you will develop his confidence and his reading ability. Time and time again teachers see the reading ability of children increase dramatically because children are reading at home.

Most children will continue to read the books in the series mentioned in Chapter 3, because they are short and deal with events in their own world. However, there are a number of 'classics' which have stood the test of time and which will take your child beyond his environment, and to which you should introduce him during this year, to show him just what can be achieved by talented writers. This should also encourage him to try new authors, styles and types of books.

If your child is of average reading ability for his age there are certain books which he should enjoy. There are a number of characters in fiction who are usually great favourites with many children at this stage in their development. These books are available in paperback, and most libraries will stock them. They include the 'Thomas the Tank Engine' books by the Rev. W. Awdry, the 'Paddington Bear' series by Michael Bond, the 'Professor Branestawm' books by Norman Hunter, the 'My Naughty Little Sister' books by Dorothy Edwards, Mary Norton's 'Borrowers' books and the 'Mrs Pepperpot' series by Alf Proysen.

If your child reads these books with ease and asks for more, he is probably ready to go on to another stage in his reading. Give him some of the books recommended in the next chapter and see how he gets on with these. On the other hand, if your child finds it difficult to get through some of the books intended for seven- to eight-year-olds then he is probably not ready for this stage yet. Encourage him to carry on reading stories which are new to him by the authors mentioned in the last chapter – Hans Andersen, the Brothers Grimm, legends and fairy tales, etc., as well as the books in the series which are probably being sent home by the school. Gently does it. Do not force your child to read books which are too hard for him, but continue to insist that he reads to an adult for at least fifteen minutes every evening. It will come, it always does. It just takes longer with some children than with others.

Poetry

This is a very good age at which to introduce your child to simple verse. It will give him considerable pleasure and will enable you to continue to work together at a number of activities.

You will probably find that your child will not want to read aloud to you at this stage. For one thing, the stories he is reading will be longer and more complex. For another, the child will regard reading as a skill which he has developed. He might be annoyed to have to continue to prove that he understands what he is reading. This is fine, it shows that he really is reading for pleasure, which is the whole point of the exercise. You and the school between you are turning your child into an independent reader. By all means chat to him about the books he is reading, but do not work out any exercises based on the story. The pair of you will have passed that stage.

Poetry is a different matter. Apart from nursery rhymes your child will probably not yet have had much to do with verse. If you can read to him or get him to read for himself the right sort of short poems and arouse his interest in them there are still plenty of things you can do together to develop his reading skills.

There are a number of poets who produce verse which really appeals to seven- to eight-year-olds. The limericks of Edward Lear go down well, as do the nonsense poems of Spike Milligan. These provide plenty of opportunities for your child to investigate the poems and then produce his own work. Give him some of the poems to read and see if he can answer questions about them and try his own hand at writing similar verse.

Limericks

There was an old man in a tree,
Who was horribly bored by a bee
When they said, 'Does it buzz?'
He replied, 'Yes it does!
It's a regular brute of a bee!'
                              (Edward Lear)

Learn the poem and say it aloud.
Can you think of another word which you could use in line two instead of 'bored'?
What other creatures could the old man have met up in the tree?
Draw a picture of the man in the tree.
How can bees be dangerous?
Work together to see if between you you can devise a new line for the last line of the limerick.

Listings

If your child is like most other children he will remain rooted permanently in front of a television set if you let him. Utilise this obsession by giving him one of the listings magazines – *Radio Times*, etc. At the beginning of the week go through it page by page with your child. You probably have a list of the programmes you allow him to watch. Make it a condition that he can watch the agreed programmes if he can show them to you on the page, read the descriptions and work out what times they are going to be shown. Then, as a writing activity, ask your child to produce his own weekly timetable of the programmes he is going to watch.

Talking and listening

Continue to talk and listen to your child, encouraging him to listen and respond intelligently. As he grows older he will be increasing the number and variety of people he meets and developing his vocabulary and approach to the needs of different audiences and situations. Without being too pedantic about it this is the time gently and occasionally to correct the grammar he is using, for example, not 'me and him,' but 'he and I', etc. Do not overdo this or your child will give up talking to you altogether, but the occasional tactful correction will be helpful and useful. Almost without seeming to know it your child will be making great strides in his ability to express himself at this stage; it is as much a part of his social development as his learning curve.

Ways of speaking and listening

You may not be able to teach your child a great deal about speaking and listening at this age, but you can perform an invaluable service by quietly monitoring and assessing his progress and putting him in positions in which he has to use and adapt his ability to listen and respond appropriately. There are a number of important signs to watch out for. You can do this just by observing your child in and out of the house.

Asking questions

Is your child asking clear and concise questions? He should be able to formulate in his mind what is puzzling or concerning him and put the problems into simple questions without any prompting. 'Where do birds go at night?' 'Why does it get dark?', etc. He will stop asking these questions if he discovers that you do not answer them or only seem to give them perfunctory attention. No matter how distracting it may be to have a small child rattling on non-stop at your side, you can at least console yourself with the thought that by answering even the most inconsequential questions in a courteous and reasoned manner you are significantly helping in his development and are providing him with an example of how to listen and reply under pressure! If your replies only trigger off more questions this is a good thing, because it should mean that your child is following up the initial questions with logical extensions, a sure sign that he is mastering the basics of language and is making good progress in English.

Talking formally

Can your child talk formally to an audience on a variety of subjects? This audience may consist only of yourself, but you could also from time to time enlist the aid of elder brothers and sisters, grandparents, etc. Try to get your child to talk to you in a sensible and controlled manner about something which interests him – his friends, games he plays, and so on. Does he seem to be marshalling his thoughts, increasing his vocabulary in order to select the right word or phrase for the occasion? The more practice he gets, the better he will become at this. Even if he is only talking about a television programme it will show that he is learning to observe, listen and repeat what he has learned. Do not interrupt him when he is talking to others; this will dent his self-confidence and make him less willing to try next time.

Talking to friends

Unobtrusively watch your child as he is playing with friends. See if he seems to be talking informally but clearly to his peers on different subjects. Is he contributing usefully to their discussions, without monopolising the conversation or, on the other hand, retiring into his shell? Do the others seem to listen to his remarks and accept them? Does he listen attentively to what they say in their turn? If he is playing normally, using language as a way of developing the games and activities, then he is using yet another tool of language in an effective manner, and all the one-to-one work you did with him as an infant and in this first year of the juniors is beginning to take effect.

Descriptions

See how easily your child can use different ways of talking about the same thing. Can he switch his language or approach in order to make something clearer? For example, if he says something is 'nice', respond to his remarks by asking him what he means by that word. See if he can select another adjective which describes the object or event more quickly. Instead of 'It was a nice party,' see if he can rephrase the sentence as 'It was a happy party,' or 'It was a noisy party,' to give a clearer picture of what the event was like. Try this with a variety of subjects as often as you can, not as an obvious lesson but as a genuine attempt to get to know what your child means. If he knows that you are really interested in what he is telling you he should try all the harder to make his meaning clear.

Writing

Throughout this year the teacher will again be following the outline of the National Curriculum. This covers:

- trying to get the children to understand and enjoy the purposes of writing – to communicate, make notes, compile lists, etc.;
- presenting them with new ideas and situations, in the hope that these will encourage the children to write – What might happen if . . . ? What would you do in this situation . . . ? etc.;
- trying to get them to organise and present their writing in different ways – diaries, lists, notes, instructions, etc.;
- planning and revising their writing – making notes and outlines, and then revising.

The help of the teacher at school and your own help as a parent at home will be essential if your child's writing is to be more than a mere exercise. Your enthusiasm is essential if your child is to regard the act of creative writing as worthwhile. Take a genuine interest in anything that your child writes and discuss it with him to show that you regard it as important. If your child's writing is of significance to you, then it will be the same to him and he will want to do as well at it as he can.

This is an age at which your child will often scribble things down at home as he masters the basics of writing, so there are a number of ways in which you can help him become an even better writer. By the time he is well in to his first junior school he should have grasped enough of the basics of grammar and punctuation to be able to write fairly freely. These basics will not at the moment consist of much more than the ability to write consecutive sentences, but when you think that this has been achieved from scratch in only a couple of years, it does give some sign of the rate at which young children progress if they have the confidence which comes from being well taught at school and helped at home.

Writing about actions

Your child should be able to write about what he is doing at the moment or what he has done in the past. He should by now have the confidence to write about things with which he is familiar.

Writing topics

Keep a diary over a period of one month.

Design and draw a cover for the diary.

Can you remember your first day at school? Write down what you can remember about it.

Write about some of the places you hurry to in order to get there, and some of the places where you walk slowly on the way.

Write about your route on the way to school.

Describe the home you live in.

Responding to new events

Your child should now be regarding writing as a tool which can be used to express his feelings as well as to record what has happened to him. The two can be combined if you can persuade him now and again to write about some new things in his life. What are these new things and how is he responding to them? Suggest he writes about any of the following: new friends, new places, new teachers, new subjects at school, new buildings, new journeys, new books, new pets, new food, new furniture, new games, new year, or new term.

Fantasy

This is a time in which many children respond eagerly to fantasy – books, videos, television programmes about witches, warlocks, bizarre countries, incredible animals and so on. The more imaginative among them enjoy writing their own fantastic stories if they are given the initial impetus, like being asked to write about a fantastic voyage, an incredible happening, and so on. If you notice your child reading such a book challenge him to match some of the incredible events in it.

For example, see if your child can find and read any books which contain magic spells. These could include *Well Met by Witchlight,* by Nina Beachcroft, *Catweazle and the Magic Zodiac,* by Richard Carpenter, *The Puffin Book of Magic Verse,* edited by Charles Causley, etc. Ask him to make up his own story about someone casting a spell. Suggest he writes it twice, first as if told by the person casting the spell, and then from the point of view of the person upon whom the spell has been cast. Ask him to write down the most blood-curdling spell he can think of and to illustrate it with pictures. He could then make up a story about a wizard or witch who loses the gift of being able to cast spells, or he could design and make a special box in which a wizard could keep his spells.

The mechanics of writing

To follow the course of the National Curriculum the teacher this year will revise the activities of the previous year and go on to see that the children:

- are beginning to use commas in sentences, as well as capital letters, question marks and full stops;
- are using joined letters in their handwriting;
- are developing their spelling ability to include the correct spelling of some words with more than one syllable.

You can help your child when he writes stories at home by checking that he is using simple sentences correctly, with capital letters, full stops and question marks in the correct places. Point out any mistakes. Your child will be expected to learn how and when to use a comma this year, so by the second term check that he understands *when* to use a comma correctly and that he is including it where necessary in his sentences and that a comma is used usually to separate words in a list, unless the word 'and' already does this. For example, 'He collected stamps, coins, post-cards and pictures.' 'She gave away apples, pears, grapes and peaches.' Encourage your child to continue to make lists, this time using sentences and inserting commas in the right places.

Handwriting

In most schools the children will have started to join their letters towards the end of Key Stage 1. This is known as *cursive* writing. This will be revised at the beginning of Key Stage 2 and the children will be expected to use joined writing for all their writing activities.

The type of joined writing being taught will certainly need to be checked with the teacher. In most schools today the children are expected to do little more than develop a neat and legible standard of handwriting. Some schools, however, go a little further using one of a number of styles, or variations or combinations of them.

Types of joined writing

Cursive: this is a basic, attractive form of handwriting notable for its use of flowing curves.

John and Mary went out.

Italic: this is characterised by its slopes and the 'thicks' and 'thins' of the lettering, caused by the angle at which the nib is used.

John and Mary went out.

Marion Richardson: this style was developed by an inspector of Art in London schools. It is based on easy and natural movements of the hand and arm.

John and Mary went out.

When a teacher begins to show children how to join their letters she will usually use the simplest possible methods at first. Ask your child's teacher if she has a handwriting pattern you can borrow, showing how she is teaching joined writing, so that you can help at home.

Grammar

When you are reading any written work produced by your child continue to check that he is using sensible short sentences, each with a capital letter, full stop and verb, and that he knows when to use question marks, and is beginning to use commas to separate words in lists.

Help him to understand that words can be used for different purposes and that they can be grouped into different sets or types. By this stage his general reading should be giving him a basic fund of information, which he ought to be able to reproduce when you question him. Make these question-and-answer sessions games, not grim homework sessions, but encourage your child to answer in complete sentences, not single words. For example: What names do we give to the homes of these creatures – person, dog, rabbit, pig, bird, bee, horse, mouse, spider. Give words which mean the opposite of – up, sell, back, in, alive, clean, dry, open, quiet, lost, hot, high, sweet, good, long, fat, near, bent.

Spelling

The more your child reads the better his spelling should become, but he will still need plenty of practice in learning words and looking up their meanings. Buy him a child's simple dictionary, and encourage him to look up the meanings of words. If the required word is not in that dictionary then use an adult's one and the pair of you can hunt for the word and its meaning together.

Combinations
Learn groups of words which have similar combinations of letters:
–alk talk, stalk, walk, chalk;
–oil boil, toil, soil, foil;
–ow bow, cow, how, low, now, mow, row;
–est best, rest, crest, vest, jest, pest, lest, nest.

Homonyms
Help your child appreciate the richness of the English language by encouraging him to learn the meanings of and to spell *homonyms* – words which sound the same but which have different spellings and meanings, for example:

blue – blew	for – four	sea – see
dear – deer	sew – so	ate – eight
etc.		

National Curriculum mathematics

During this year the teacher will follow the National Curriculum requirements and:

• revise and consolidate the work done at Key Stage 1;

- work with numbers up to 1000, using calculators and computers where appropriate, and develop an understanding of multiplication and division;
- work increasingly with shapes and begin to understand and use measures;
- start to work with *data*, for example, information involving the use of diagrams, graphs, etc.

You may think at first that your child is not making much progress in mathematics in Year 3. There are several reasons for this. In the first place the children will just have returned from a long summer holiday. They may well have forgotten some of the basic skills they developed at Key Stage 1. For the first month or so the teacher will be revising the work done in the infant classes until she is satisfied that they are capable of going on to the next stage.

Another reason for an apparent lack of progress in the first term is that the kind of mathematics being used by the children is changing. At Key Stage 1 a great deal of the work undertaken will have been practical, involving the use of counters, beads, games and so on. For the course of Key Stage 2, there will still be many practical activities, but there will also be more abstract and theoretical work for the children to understand. You can help your child at home by continuing to let him see you using maths in your everyday life, but you can also help considerably if you make sure that he understands the basic skills and concepts which he is being taught at school over this year.

Number

Make sure that your child can understand numbers up to 1000. Write down examples of these numbers and see if he can identify or 'read' them – 567, 789, 980, etc. If you can, help him to visualise large numbers by showing him examples of them. Show him thousands of people attending a football match on a television programme. As he begins to gain confidence ask him to *estimate* or guess the number of sweets in a jar, the number of buttons in a container, etc. Count these with him and see how close his estimate was.

Hundreds, tens and units
Your child should be beginning to understand the difference in place values of hundreds tens and units. Help him with this by giving him a set of three-figure numbers, for example, 146, 767, 895, and so on. Ask him to tell you how much each figure is worth. In 895, for example, the 8 is eight hundreds, the 9 is nine tens, and the 5 is five units. Keep on with this exercise until your child can identify place values straight away. As he gains in confidence let him do addition of hundreds, tens and units, carrying figures over from one column to another.

Multiplication

Go on to help your child understand what multiplication is. He may have already grasped the concept at school, but if you make sure that he knows what he is doing you can then go on to other things. If he still seems puzzled by the idea keep practising with him.

Use counters and a series of ten trays, saucers or plates (polystyrene food trays from the supermarket could be used). Tell your child that you are going to look at the tables he already knows – $2 \times$, $4 \times$, $5 \times$ – in order to *multiply*.

Start with the $2 \times$ table. Place two counters or buttons in each of the ten trays. Ask your child to collect four lots of 2s. Explain that we can write this as 4×2. Ask your child to count the counters and say how many the four sets of 2 come to. Carry on with five sets of 2 and so on. Do the same with $4 \times$ and $5 \times$ tables.

Give your child some simple sums to do involving these three tables – 6×2, 7×4, 8×5, etc. Ask him to do these sums, using his knowledge of the appropriate tables, but to check the answers by taking the appropriate numbers of counters from the trays and checking the answers in this way.

After a time your child will associate the practical grouping of counters with the abstract idea of multiplying figures on paper. This will give him a solid basis in his understanding of multiplication. Give him practice in this throughout the year, especially when he begins to learn new tables at school.

Table squares

A valuable aid to the understanding of multiplication and the use of tables is the *table square*. Let your child gradually build up his own table square over the year, filling it in as he masters different tables. This will help your child to understand how numbers can be moved and manipulated in a logical way. An outline of a table square will look like this:

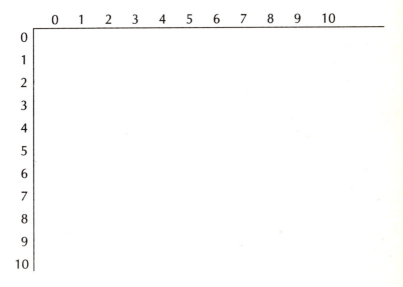

A young child will soon realise that anything multiplied by nought remains nought, and that anything multiplied by one remains the same. This means that as soon as he has learnt his 2 × table he can fill in the first three lines of the table – 0 ×, 1 × and 2 ×:

	0	1	2	3	4	5	6	7	8	9	10
0	0	0	0								
1	0	1	2								
2	0	2	4								
3	0	3	6								
4	0	4	8								
5	0	5	10								
6	0	6	12								
7	0	7	14								
8	0	8	16								
9	0	9	18								
10	0	10	20								

When your child has learned the 3 × table he can fill in the next line down, and so on. By the end of this year most children will be expected to know their 2 ×, 3 ×, 4 × and 5 × tables. By the time they complete Key Stage 2 they should know their tables up to 10.

A completed table square is shown below. To use the table square, all a child has to do if he wants to find, say, 7 × 8, is to find the number 7 working down the left hand column, and then run his finger along that line until it comes to the column under the number 8 in the top row. The number which is in line with the 7 and under the 8 is the answer, for example, 56 (7 × 8 = 56). Let your child have plenty of practice doing this. A completed table should look like this:

	0	1	2	3	4	5	6	7	8	9	10
0	0	0	0	0	0	0	0	0	0	0	0
1	0	1	2	3	4	5	6	7	8	9	10
2	0	2	4	6	8	10	12	14	16	18	20
3	0	3	6	9	12	15	18	21	24	27	30
4	0	4	8	12	16	20	24	28	32	36	40
5	0	5	10	15	20	25	30	35	40	45	50
6	0	6	12	18	24	32	36	42	48	54	60
7	0	7	14	21	28	35	42	49	56	63	70
8	0	8	16	24	32	40	48	56	64	72	80
9	0	9	18	27	36	45	54	63	72	81	90
10	0	10	20	30	40	50	60	70	80	90	100

Division

The last important aspect of number which the teacher will introduce this year will probably be that of division. Some children find this difficult to understand at first, but there are a number of ways in which you can help at home.

The most effective way of helping at home is to see that your child understands the principle of *sharing*. Put him into a position where he has to make practical decisions – 'How can we share these twenty sweets among the five people in the house, so that each person gets the same number?' 'We have got eight pieces of cake to share among four people. How can we do that fairly?'

If you spend a few weeks doing this, your child should have little difficulty in going on to working out division sums with a paper and pencil.

Calculator activities

Get your child to use a calculator to check his answers to addition, subtraction, multiplication and division sums.
Count on in twos and fours to reinforce knowledge of tables and number patterns.

Measuring

Your child should have had a good grounding in the principles of measuring at Key Stage 1, using non-standard measures. This year the teacher will be introducing him to *standard* measures. This will involve using a ruler to measure centimetres and half-centimetres, and weighing objects in the classroom. You can help here by making sure that your child can use a ruler and understands where and how the centimetres are marked on it. If you also let him see you weighing things in the kitchen this will help him understand the importance of measuring accurately and will show him the different ways of measuring, for example, dry goods and liquids.

Shape, space and measures

Anything that you can do at home to make your child think about shapes and space and measuring them will be of great use in the work he does at school. Here are some practical activities to do at home:

- Use a real compass to teach your child the four main points – north, south, east and west. Work out the directions of landmarks from your garden. Play games involving giving and following instructions, for example, 'Walk twenty paces to the east,' etc.
- When helping your child to tell the time, use a clockface with moveable hands to introduce the concepts of *clockwise* and *anti-clockwise*.
- Use a piece of string to mark out a straight line in the garden to plant seeds. Discuss how the string helps to produce the straight line.

Handling data

Help your child to understand how different simple pieces of equipment provide us with information. Use a thermometer to note and record the temperature each day. Read digital clocks and compare the times with those on watches with hands. Compare the weights of different objects and estimate the respective weights. Then use a pair of scales to check the answers.

Problems

> *Why do we have to bother with all these practical maths activities? Couldn't the children just learn their tables and get on with it, like they used to do?*

A lot of parents and some teachers would agree whole-heartedly with this. It does make the whole process of teaching and learning maths much easier if it is all done by memorising a few techniques and then using them to solve problems. This is a process which would suit a few children with good memories quite well, but for the vast majority of boys and girls it makes mathematics a misery. If children can relate the questions in the book before them to the measuring they have done in a corner of the playground then it really does help them to come to grips with the subject.

National Curriculum science

In Year 3 the teacher will continue to help your child to:

- think and act in a scientific manner;
- plan experimental work;
- obtain and consider evidence.

He will continue to explore the scientific areas looked at in the previous year:

- life processes and living things;
- materials and their properties;
- physical processes.

Help your child by giving him chances to explore science in everyday life, investigating, enquiring and communicating his findings, taking into account the hazards and risks in such work and observing health and safety precautions.

Life processes and living things

Help your child to discover more about his body and the way in which it works. Try out this heart experiment with your child to see how the action of the heart pumps blood through the body: Feel your pulse, either at the wrist or the side of the neck. There are *arteries* here through which the blood is being pumped away from the heart. How many times does your heart beat in one minute? Compare this with other people at home. Now play an energetic game or take some exercise, and count how many times your heart beats in one minute now. The heart beats faster after exercise, so the pulse-rate should be higher.

Now try out this muscle experiment. Our muscles enable us to move, and our movements are controlled by our muscles. A muscle is made up of a group of strands called *fibres,* and these fibres become shorter and fatter when they are moved. This is called *contracting* a muscle. Get your child to lift something up, bending his elbow as far as it will go. What happens to the biceps muscle in his upper arm?

A bone collection

The bones in a body give it its shape. They also shelter and protect the soft parts of the body, such as the heart and lungs. The bones of the body together are known as the *skeleton.* See how many different kinds of animal bones you can find. Collect them, clean them, label them and put them on display. (Do remember to get your child to wash his hands well after handling bones.)

Materials and their properties

Help your child to make a study of the different materials around him, how they are made and what they are used for. Perhaps you could help him to make a brick. For a long time people used stones to make houses. Then they started making bricks. These were better than stones because they were all the same shape and could be placed on top of one another. Help your child to make a brick by mixing some clay with a little sand. Shape it in the form of a brick. Dry it in the sun, on a radiator, or in the oven. Examine the finished brick. Does it look all right? If anything goes wrong with the first effort, try to make another, using any information you have learned in the construction of the first one.

Physical processes

Examine different shaped magnets with your child. Show him examples of the horseshoe-shaped magnets and the straight ones. Say that they each work in the same way. Explain that the Earth acts like a magnet. The North Pole attracts certain metals, which will point in the direction of the Pole (although the magnetic Pole is not quite in the same position as the geographical one). Because of this people have been able to develop a compass, with a needle which will always point to the north.

National Curriculum design and technology

During this year, the teacher will:

- revise the previous year's skills and activities;
- encourage children to generate their own ideas;
- think about the order in which they are going to do their work, choosing tools and materials carefully.

Continue to help your child to feel at home using simple tools, and to understand that in order for things to be made to higher standards they should be planned, built with the right materials, tested and, where necessary, altered. Try to encourage him to make his own simple and useful models, coming to you for advice if he cannot see the next step in any of his work. These models could include making a simple pair of book-ends, or a draught-excluder for the door of his bedroom.

A wind station

Plan and make a simple wind station for use in the garden. Start by deciding what sorts of equipment will be needed. A basic station could include a *vane*, to judge the direction of the wind and a *windsock* to show the direction and strength of the wind.
Select materials, tools and techniques.

For a vane, a base will be needed on to which a pole or stick will be attached. On top of the stick a pin could be stuck, and a cardboard arrow attached to the pin.

For the windsock one end of a sock should be cut off. This end of the sock should be attached by strings to a pole. Wire should be placed round the inside of the hole at the other end of the sock, to keep it open. A strong wind will catch the sock and blow through it.

Plan these pieces of equipment and draw diagrams showing what they will look like. Devise tests for the finished models and make any necessary changes.

National Curriculum history

Over the four years of Key Stage 2 the children will study a number of set periods of history in the National Curriculum:

- Romans, Anglo-Saxons and Vikings in Britain;
- Life in Tudor times;
- Victorian Britain *or* Britain since 1930;
- Ancient Greece;
- Local history;
- A past non-European society (chosen from Ancient Egypt, Mesopotamia, the Indus Valley, the Maya, Benin, the Aztecs).

It is left to the school to decide in which order these subjects should be studied, and how they should be organised over the school year.

If you discover from your child's class teacher which particular period is being covered in a given year, you could help in a number of practical ways by showing him examples of the period in question. If the Romans are being examined, then a visit to a Roman wall, or a display at a local museum will be helpful. If the Vikings are the subject of the curriculum then a visit to the great Viking exhibition in York will bring the period to life for your child.

However, do not be tempted to do much more than this to help with the specific period being covered at school. Instead, continue to keep your child's interest in the whole subject of history alive. Over this year you could just show him how we know what we do about the past. Help him to discover the many different ways of finding out about the past, for example, from:

- books;
- pictures;
- buildings;
- old tools and weapons;
- rocks and fossils;
- the memories of older people;
- museums and collections;
- myths and legends;
- clothes, etc.

Anything that you can do to help your child discover that the past was different from the present, but that it is possible to discover what happened before he was born, will help him enormously to get to grips with the difficult idea of past and present. Take him to museums, working out in advance which particular aspects of the display you are going to concentrate on, ask older members of the family to discuss their own memories, compare modern tools with older ones, look at old buildings and talk about who used to live there and how they lived. Tell him how things have changed in your lifetime, and ask his grandparents to do the same. At this stage anything which makes your child think about the passing of time and how we can see evidence of it all around us will be very helpful in his getting to grips with the subject of history.

These outings need not nor should not take the form of an intensive outward-bound course, but if you can manage to take your child out to places of interest four or five times in the course of a year this will back up the work being done at school to cover the history curriculum.

National Curriculum geography

Over the course of Key Stage 2 the teacher will be:

- investigating places in general and the children's own locality in particular, together with two other areas, one in the United Kingdom and one overseas;
- increasing the children's geographical knowledge of such places as rivers, mountains, valleys, etc.;
- investigating the weather and what causes different conditions;
- looking at settlements, like towns, cities, villages, etc.;
- studying changes in the environment.

Not all these areas will be covered in one year; the teachers will select aspects to be studied over each year of Key Stage 2 in order to cover the requirements of the National Curriculum.

You can help your child at home by looking at different aspects of your own locality and encouraging him to take an interest in the geographical aspects of the area around your home. If you help him to study one or two themes over the course of the year he will bring into play the geographical knowledge and skills he is learning at school.

It would be silly to suppose that the world is full of eager little boys and girls straining at the leash to be allowed to go out to undertake local investigations, complete with clip-boards and project sheets, but it should be possible to arouse the occasional flicker of interest in the locality in your child and to respond to this and get him thinking in a geographical manner. You will not have time, and your child almost certainly will not have the inclination, for any intensive projects, but if you can arouse the interest of your child in one or two local aspects of the area in which he lives, and persuade him to want to find out a little about his surroundings, it all helps!

Local shops and supermarkets

Look at the shops and supermarkets in your area.

Mapping: make a map of the main shops.

Change: how do these shops change over time? Do some open and others close? Do new shops spring up? Are open spaces used for the building of new stores? Why do you think these changes take place?

Goods: What do the shops sell? Do any of the goods come from the locality, for example, fruit, vegetables, etc., or are they brought in from far away?

Distances: are all the shops in the same general locality, or are they scattered over a wider area? Why do you think the shops are placed where they are?

Transport: what forms of transport are used to bring goods to the shop? Do they all come by road, or do some come by rail? How do the different trucks and lorries differ. Can you see from the inscriptions on the lorries where they come from?

Other local projects which could be studied include: buildings, transport, water, weather, pollution, etc.

National Curriculum art

The teacher will continue to help her children to develop in the two main areas of art:

- investigating and making;
- knowledge and understanding.

Over this year children will become more dextrous and ambitious. They will want to increase their range of skills. You can help at home by showing your child one or two simple artistic skills within his range, and by encouraging him to practise them. It does not matter whether or not your child has been shown these techniques at school. What you are doing is showing him that there are all sorts of new things to be learnt in art, and that most of them are not difficult to master. There are a number of techniques which your child should be able to cope with after a little encouragement. Let him display the results on the wall of his bedroom, or use them for family birthday cards, etc. Here are a few examples.

Candlewax pictures
Draw a simple picture, using a candle instead of a pencil. Cover the sheet of paper with a dark poster paint and allow it to dry. The wax picture should show through clearly.

Fabric collage
Make a fabric collage of a figure. Choose the figure you wish to make from pictures in books. You could try to make a Roman soldier, or a prehistoric person, a modern figure, or anyone else. Copy the picture on to a large piece of cardboard and cut it out in anatomical sections – head and shoulders, torso, arms, legs, etc.

Now collect different kinds of fabric, and place a different piece under each cut-out section of the body. Cut the fabrics into the shapes of the sections, and then select a large piece of plain cloth for the background. Pin the cut-out pieces of fabric on to this background, marking the position of each piece lightly with a pencil. Use a latex adhesive to stick each section of the figure into position on the backing cloth, and then pad all over with a cloth.

Watercolour resist
Draw a picture in crayon on good quality paper. Wash watercolour paint over the drawing. The crayoned picture should stand out as the crayon resists the watercolour.

Junk jewellery
Look at examples of jewellery, and then try to make some out of scrap materials and junk. Collect and grade nails according to their length. Clean and polish them and knot them on to a length of string or some other support. Place the shortest nails in the middle, flanked by the longer ones. Can the necklace be made more attractive by covering the string with foil?

Other techniques suitable for this age include making sculptures from wire, sticking lengths of string over a pattern, covering drawings of buildings with layers of matchsticks stuck on to them, making figures from silver foil, and making sand paintings by mixing sand with water and tempera paint until the correct consistency of paint has been attained.

National Curriculum music

The teacher will be increasing the range of the music listened to, assessed and performed by the children. Over the course of this year she will help the children to:

- perform accurately and confidently;
- sing songs with attack and enjoyment;
- listen to and enjoy suitable music.

The teacher may not use the actual technical terms involved, but throughout this year she will be trying to instil in the children a number of basic techniques of music. You can help your child at home with these.

Techniques

Pitch: use a number of different simple instruments and see if their sounds can be made higher or lower. Listen to everyday noises and categorise them as *high* and *low*.

Pace: can some noises made with the voice be made quicker or slower? Make lists of noises around you and list them as *fast* and *slow*.

Texture: try to combine different noises to make a pleasant sound. Work with your child, one strumming notes on a guitar, the other looking for similar notes on a piano. Can you hear any mixtures of sounds around you? Are they pleasant or unpleasant sounds?

Timbre: compare the quality of sound made by different instruments. Describe the sounds being made.

Dynamics: distinguish loud sounds and quiet sounds. Listen to songs and passages of music, some of which are loud, and some of which are quiet.

National Curriculum physical education

Over Key Stage 2, teachers will continue to ask their children to take place in activities which come under the heading of 'Dance, gymnastics and games'. They will also introduce new aspects of physical education:

- swimming (may be undertaken at KS 1);
- athletic activities (running, jumping, throwing);
- outdoor and athletic activities (including solving problems, alone and with others) in different environments – camping, walking, expeditions, etc.

A new area of physical education is outdoor and adventurous activities. These will involve the children in a number of projects involving the environment – walking, tracking, climbing, etc. All these activities will be carefully supervised, but this is an age at which children like to take chances. You will help the teacher considerably in many areas of physical education if you can impress upon him the importance of taking normal health and safety precautions before, during and after these activities.

Health and Safety precautions

Always warm up before taking part in any physical activities.
Always take time to cool down after physical activities.
Always consider other children while taking part in activities.
If there are rules to a game or activity, make sure that they are followed.
Always concentrate and try to perform every movement as efficiently as possible.
Make sure that you know and observe the Highway Code.
Make sure that you know what to do if there is a fire drill at school.

Take great care when handling any physical education equipment.
Get to know any dangerous sections of the road near your home and school and how to cross them safely.

End of Year 3 checklists

Most, but not all children should be able to meet the majority of these targets by the end of Year 3. They should also still be able to meet the requirements set for the end of Key Stage 1 given at the end of Chapter 3.

English

Speaking and listening
The child:

- can ask clear and sensible questions;
- can follow up these questions logically;
- can answer questions in clear, concise sentences;
- can talk formally to different audiences on a variety of subjects;
- can talk informally and clearly to his friends, and contribute to their discussions;
- can find alternative ways of describing the same thing;
- can show a steady development in his spoken vocabulary;
- can listen to a story and answer questions about it;
- can follow instructions efficiently.

Reading
The child:

- is beginning to select books for himself, to read both for pleasure and information;
- is beginning to have favourite books;
- is able to read longer books, putting them down and taking them up again;

- is beginning to read some poetry;
- can use reading as a practical aid, for example, to discover the time of a television programme, etc.

Writing
The child:

- can produce different forms of writing – stories, descriptions, accounts of events, etc.;
- can use writing to describe his reaction to new things;
- is beginning to enjoy writing about the fantastic and things outside his experience.

Grammar
The child can write confidently in sentences containing capital letters, full stops, commas and, where necessary, question marks.

Handwriting
The child can write legibly using a form of joined handwriting.

Spelling
The child can spell an increasing range of words, including some with more than one syllable.

Mathematics

Number
The child:

- can recognise numbers up to 1000;
- can distinguish between hundreds, tens and units;
- can add and subtract tens and units;
- can divide and multiply units and, in some cases, tens and units;
- is beginning to use standard measures;
- can use table squares;
- knows the 2 ×, 3 ×, 4 × and 5 × tables.

YEAR 3 – AGES SEVEN TO EIGHT

Shape, space and measures
The child knows the main points of the compass, and understands the meanings of *clockwise* and *anti-clockwise*.

Handling data
The child is beginning to understand and use mechanisms which provide information, for example, thermometers, digital watches, etc.

Science

Life processes and living things
The child understands the uses and functions in the human body of the heart, lungs, muscles, nerves, blood-system and bones.

Materials and their properties
The child understands the uses of different materials and how to test these materials.

Physical processes
The child understands about magnetism.

Design and technology

Designing skills
The child:

- can see what needs to be done;
- can communicate to others what needs to be done;
- can make a design to cover what needs to be done.

Making skills
The child:

- is beginning to develop a number of making skills, including: cutting and assembling, weaving, clay modelling, stick printing, paper folding, shaping, papier mâché work;
- can devise increasingly effective tests for what has been designed and made.

History

The child:

- is beginning to understand and use different sources to discover more about the past;
- is beginning to understand the idea of *chronology*, the idea that events happened in a certain order in history, starting with the first creatures on earth.

Geography

The child:

- is taking an interest in aspects of his own locality;
- understands that there have been many changes on earth over the century;
- knows that people gather together in *settlements*;
- understands that climate and weather can have an effect upon the way in which people live;
- knows about some of the major landforms – mountains, hills, deserts, rivers, valleys, seas, etc.

Art

Investigating and making

The child is beginning to experiment with new techniques and tools, including drawing, candle patterns, wax-resist, crayon pictures, painting, dyeing, finger painting, junk sculptures, wire constructions, collages, sand painting, silver foil work, string and matchstick patterns, etc.

Knowledge and understanding

The child is beginning to take an interest in the artwork of others and to use their techniques in his own work.

Music

Performing and composing

The child:

- is singing and beginning to play simple musical instruments;

- is making music with others as well as on his own;
- is using music in conjunction with drama, dance and movement.

Listening and appraising

The child:

- is listening to an increasing range of music;
- understands the meaning of some basic musical terms;
- can talk about the music he enjoys.

Physical Education

The child is approaching physical activities sensibly, with consideration for others and an awareness of health and safety factors.

Parents and teachers talking

There are different ways of telling that your child is growing up. He gets taller, he makes more noise – and his school work gets a lot harder for his parents to cope with.

You certainly learn a lot about your children when you work at home with them. I have discovered that my daughter is absolutely steadfast in her self-belief, even when she is wrong! The number of dead-ends she has confidently led me down in our maths work! Talk about the blind leading the blind!

I wanted to help my boy with his music, so I asked him what sort of hymns and songs they sang in assembly. According to him the answer was hardly any. Apparently the headmaster is an inter-schools swimming organiser, and he's always talking about the results of matches. His assemblies seem to be five minutes with the Lord and fifteen with the backstroke. So that wasn't much help with the music. ,

, *As a young and enthusiastic class teacher I really wanted to launch a scheme to involve all the parents in helping their children with the National Curriculum at home. I wanted one particularly aggressive and domineering mum to act as liaison officer, so I went up to her at the school gate and told her what I wanted. I ended by trying to use a little flattery, saying, "I've chosen you because you're so independent, decisive and tough-minded." She looked worried and replied, "I don't know, I'll have to ask my husband!"* ,

Useful books for seven- to eight-year-olds

English

(Reading books)

The Iron Man, Ted Hughes (Faber)
Fantastic Mr Fox, Roald Dahl (Young Puffin)
The Little Grey Men, 'BB' (Methuen)
Mooninsummer Madness, Tove Jansson (Puffin)
Stig of the Dump, Clive King (Puffin)
Fattypuffs and Thinnifers, Andre Maurois (Bodley Head)
The Big Egg, William Mayne (Hamilton)

(Collections of poetry)

A First Poetry Book, John Foster (ed.) (OUP)
Starlight, Starbright, Anne Harvey (ed.) (Julia Macrae)
Pilly Soems, Michael Rosen (ed.) (A and C Black)

Mathematics

Starting Points series, Andrew Parker and Jane Stamford (Schofield and Sims)
Table Trails, Charles Cuff (Longman)

Science

A First Look... series (*Science and Materials, Science and Ourselves*, etc.), Cyril Gilbert and Peter Matthews (Longman)
Search Out Science, Mary Horn, Ann Orchard, Beryl Peters, Gill Gething, Fen Marshall and Diane Ward (Longman)

Design and Technology

An Early Start to Technology Through Science, Roy Richards (Simon and Schuster)

History

The Ancient Greeks, Pat Taylor (Heinemann)
Cross-Sections series (*Man-of-War, Castle*, etc.), Stephen Biesty (Dorling Kindersley)

Geography

Going Places series (*Where People Live, Where People Shop*, etc.), Barbara Taylor (A and C Black)
Roundabouts (*The Ground Below Us, The Sky Above Us*, etc.), Kate Petty (A and C Black)

Art

Paint Craft, Maureen Roffey (Macmillan)
Paper Craft, Maureen Roffey (Macmillan)

Music

Three Singing Pigs: Making Music With Traditional Stories, Kaye Umansky (A and C Black)
High Low Dolly Pepper: Developing Music Skills With Young Children, Veronica Clark (A and C Black)
The Chappell Music Books, David Gregory (Evans)

CHAPTER SIX

Year 4 – Ages eight to nine

" They're lovely! I'd like to take them all home with me!"

(Year 4 teacher)

If primary school teachers had their choice they would like all the classes in the school to be like the one containing the eight- to nine-year-olds. This is a smashing year. The children are beginning to master most of the basic skills and techniques necessary to produce interesting results, yet they are still enthusiastic and eager to work. In many schools this is known as 'the work year', because so much gets done.

Some of the work done over this year is consolidation. The teacher is putting to use the skills the children have learned over the last few years and giving them the confidence to use these skills to produce an increasingly high standard of work. The best general thing that you can do with your child at this age is, as always, to be available and supportive. She will almost certainly be doing most of the work that needs to be done at school at this stage.

Nevertheless, there are still many new skills and techniques to be learnt. Children probably cover more ground over this school year than in any other in the primary years. Most of them become absorbed in what is happening at school, so much so that they often want to do less at home than in previous years. However, there are still plenty of things that you can do to support the teacher as she covers the ground of the National Curriculum.

National Curriculum English

Children will be expected to:

- understand the ideas and characters in the books they read, and seek and use books to provide information;
- talk and listen with confidence;
- write in a lively and thoughtful manner over a range of forms, with an ever-widening vocabulary in a fluent, joined hand-writing.

Helping with reading, speaking and listening

By this stage, thanks to the work you and the teachers have been doing, your child should be able to talk fluently and listen with understanding. There will be less need for you to put her into situations where she can talk. She ought to be looking for these situations herself and using them for her speaking and listening. If your child still seems unable or unwilling to join in group activities or is reluctant to talk to adults, have a word with the teacher and see what she thinks. The teacher will have far more opportunities than you to see how your child mixes with her peers.

You should still be making sure that your child reads as much as possible at home. Over the next year or two a number of children drift away from reading and this lack of contact with words and ideas is soon reflected in their school work. The best thing that you can do is to make sure that the right sorts of books are available at home, and hope that she will pick them up and start reading them.

This is a stage when, in addition to reading about modern children and their exploits, most boys and girls enjoy reading about heroes of legend – Robin Hood, King Arthur, Odysseus, and so on. Among modern authors they enjoy reading are Clive King, Raymond Briggs, Russell Hoban, Helen Cresswell and Mary Norton.

Try to have a good children's encyclopaedia in the house and encourage your child to look things up in it. At school this term the teacher will be encouraging her to use a variety of reference books in many different National Curriculum activities. You can also encourage your child to use reference books as a matter of course in which to look things up at home. Tell her that you want to find the addresses of several of her friends, and go through the local telephone directory with her. Involve her in planning rail and air routes if you are going on holiday. Examine holiday brochures together, and use calendars to plot forthcoming events.

Writing

At school the teacher will be encouraging her children to use their newly acquired skills to write in as many different forms as possible – stories, instructions, etc.

Your child will probably be doing so much writing at school that she will not want to do any exercises at home. However, you can keep her in practice by devising ways of using her writing ability in a variety of real-life situations. By this age she should be writing to relations and friends, thanking them for presents and responding to invitations to parties. At school she will be writing across the curriculum – accounts of science experiments, forecasts of design and technology projects, etc., so encourage her to use writing in her hobbies at home. If she collects things ask her to label them; if she is feeding her pets ask her to write down a timetable showing what she is feeding them with and when she is doing it; if she enjoys cooking ask her to keep her own recipe book, and so on.

During all this, make sure that her handwriting is joined, legible and beginning to show signs of a personal style.

The mechanics of writing

You will be able to judge your child's handwriting by looking at it when she writes her labels, recipes, lists, etc. In the area of grammar, your child's teacher will be enlarging her knowledge of language over this year by introducing her to the use of *verbs*, *nouns* and the use of *a* and *an*. She will also be adding to the number of words which your child should be able to spell. Some teachers will also be going on to the use of *singular* and *plural*.

This curriculum may sound very daunting to the average parent, but really there is not a great deal that you can do to help here. By now your child will be independent, with a developing mind of her own. She will not welcome the prospect of coming home to face a barrage of tests on the use of parts of speech, and if you tried anything like this it would normally do more harm than good. Where you can still be of help is by giving her the occasional spelling test. Children quite like these and your child should be prepared to be tested now and again.

Spelling tests

Begin to test your child on the formation of compound words – put two individual words together and form a compound word, for example, head and ache form *headache*; foot and ball can form *football*, and so on. Give your child a number of individual words and ask him to match them and write down and spell a compound word, for example, *mat*, *time*, *milk* and *man*, *door* and *home*, may be matched to form *doormat*, *milkman* and *hometime*.

National Curriculum mathematics

This year the teacher will be following the National Curriculum requirements and teaching her children to:

- apply mathematics to practical problems, present information in a clear and organised way, check results, try out own ideas;

- begin to use decimals, continue to add, subtract, multiply and divide;
- classify 2-D and 3-D shapes, measure length, capacity, mass and time in different contexts;
- interpret and use information obtained from lists, begin to use graphs and other ways of presenting information.

The National Curriculum requires a great deal of work to be done on measurements over this year. The best way in which you can help your child at home is by giving her plenty of chances to use measurements in practical ways and then associate this practical work with written mathematics.

Weighing

Encourage your child to keep a constant record of her own weight on the bathroom scales. Give her the opportunity to use all sorts of different weighing apparatus about the house, measuring quantities for cooking recipes, etc. Help her to use the standard weights of *gramme* and *kilogramme*. Ask her to compare the weights of different objects, first by estimating and then by checking on the scales, for example, 'Which will be the heavier, a packet of sugar or this jar of jam?' 'Weigh that jar of jam and work out how much three jars will weigh,' etc.

After this practical work make sure that your child knows that 100 grammes = 1 kilogramme, and that these are written down as *g* and *kg*. See if she can do some adding up sums involving different weights, giving the answers in grammes and kilogrammes.

Weight

kg	g	kg	g	kg	g	kg
	40		35		20	50
	+		+		+	+
	55		70		85	60
	—		—		—	—

Capacity

Give your child experience filling different-shaped containers, to show her how much these containers can hold. Ask her to help you in the kitchen as you fill jars with rice, biscuits, etc. First of all ask her to *estimate* or guess the size of the containers which will be needed for the different goods – 'Will all the biscuits go into that tin?', and so on. Make this more difficult by varying the sizes of the containers.

Then do the same thing with liquids, like water – 'How much water will we need to fill that bottle?', etc. The most common unit of capacity which your child will use this year will be the *litre*, so give her plenty of chances to work with this amount. Measure out litres and transfer them from one container to another. Estimate which containers will hold a litre, and how many litres larger containers may hold. Always follow up by measuring and checking estimates made.

When your child has grown accustomed to working with litres, go on to *equivalence* of litres – other quantities which are the same as a litre. Ask your child to measure out two half litres and to compare these with one litre. Give her plenty of practice with this, until she understands that two half litres are the same as one litre. Spread this work out over the course of a year.

From this go on to simple written addition, subtraction, multiplication and division sums involving litres. At this stage the teacher will not usually go on to the other units of metric capacity such as dekalitres, etc.

Shapes

Revise with your child the basic shapes – circles, squares, triangles and rectangles. Look for examples of these shapes in everyday life – windows, doors, bottle-tops, patterns, etc. Encourage her to cut out geometrical shapes from sticky coloured paper and to make them into patterns. When she seems at home with these shapes, show her new ones – especially cones, cylinders and cubes.

> **Equivalence of shapes**
>
> Experiment with *equivalence* of shapes. Using sticky coloured paper or 3-D examples of shapes, make new shapes from existing ones. Two semi-circles will make a circle. Two triangles may be joined to make a square, etc.

Tesselation

At this age you can begin to introduce your child to a study of area, or space. This is best done by activities involving *tesselation*. The true definition of tesselation means to cover an area with flat pieces of paving. In mathematics, however, it involves covering a marked area with squares or half-squares and counting these to work out the surface of an area. This is an introduction to more advanced measuring of area which will be carried out later on in the school.

If you link this with art activities you could ask your child to make mosaics out of squares or half-squares of coloured sticky paper by inserting them inside the outlines of squares and rectangles, and counting the squares and half-squares afterwards.

National Curriculum science

This year the teacher will be following the National Curriculum and helping the children to:

- conduct tests and predict what will happen;
- continue to study animals and plants;
- look at the purposes for which materials can be used and how some materials can change;
- study movement, light, electricity and friction.

Children enjoy studying the materials around them. You can help to develop their knowledge and supplement their National Curriculum work in a number of ways, working with your child in short bursts over the course of the year. Here are a few simple experiments that your child might carry out:

Chemical changes

A chemical change occurs when a new substance is made from two other substances working together. Rust is an example of chemical change.

Put some carpet tacks in a jar and sprinkle them with water. Cover the jar and leave it for a few days. The mixture of moisture and oxygen in the jar will cause rust. Look for ways of making rust, using other materials exposed to oxygen and moisture in this way. Make a study of rusty areas in your house and in the locality generally. Make maps and drawings of rusty items and areas.

Physical changes

A physical change comes about when the appearance of something changes but there has been no chemical change. Water changing to ice is a physical change, and so is water changing to steam. Experiment by putting water into an ice-box and talking and writing about what happens.

Properties of materials

The *property* of a material is how it behaves when something is done to it. Make a list of materials which bend and those which do not bend. Which materials bend the most? In what ways might it be useful for a material to bend? Look for other ways of changing materials – stretching, etc. Keep a notebook of these experiments over the year.

Purification

Some things may be changed for the better by being *purified* or made cleaner. Collect samples of dirty water from different locations, and pass each sample through a filter paper into a jar. What happens to the water passing into the jar? What is left on the filter paper? What changes have taken place.

Continue to carry out this experiment with different samples of water at intervals over the year, keeping a notebook of results and saying which are the cleanest and dirtiest samples of water. Ask your child how and why the food we eat is purified, and how we can keep food pure and free from harmful bacteria.

Testing materials
Over the course of a year collect different strips of material – cotton, denim, etc. Think of a number of tests you could use for each piece of material to find out which ones are most waterproof and which ones resist wear the best. Keep a notebook of the experiments and tests over the year.

Then, make a collection of different metals over a long period. Label them and describe them. Which ones look the best after they have been cleaned and polished? Think of appropriate tests for other materials. What are you testing for in each case?

National Curriculum design and technology

The teacher will continue to help her children to take part in a variety of designing and making assignments. Throughout the year she will encourage the children to:

- generate their own ideas, recognising that they will have to meet different requirements;
- produce step-by-step plans for their designs, identifying the tools, materials and processes required.

At home, continue to encourage your child to design and make various objects, taking increasing care with the planning and designing stages. Over the course of a year help your child to recognise that everyday mechanical objects have to be designed and made by showing her some of the domestic appliances about the house and seeing if she can make her own working models of a number of these. For example, show your child a picture of a pair of bellows. Explain that these were used to fan the embers of a dying fire and bring them back to life. See if your child can make a model of working bellows from an empty squeezy bottle or a balloon, or something similar. Why don't we use pairs of bellows today?

See if your child can plan, design and make any other working models of kitchen equipment over the year, for example, a piece of pressing apparatus which will squeeze the moisture out of washing, a pair of weighing scales or a clothes-horse, etc.

National Curriculum history

The teacher will continue to concentrate on one of the periods of history suggested in the National Curriculum – Ancient Greeks, Britain since 1930, etc. In addition, she will be trying to arouse the interest and awareness of the children in a number of aspects of history. She will help the children to understand that:

- the past can be divided into different periods of time;
- certain events and people from each of these periods were of more importance than others;
- there are reasons for changes and events in history.

If you know which particular period your child is studying, you can help her by providing her with books about it and taking her on visits to places of interest. On a more general level, by chatting to her and giving her stories to read, you can also help her to think and talk about some of the more important concepts or ideas of history which she must grasp if she is to understand the subject properly. Some of these concepts include:

Struggle
From the beginning of time people have struggled to survive and to better their living conditions. Stories which emphasise this include the efforts of prehistoric people as hunters, the effort of Noah and his family to escape the flood, the struggles of the Vikings to farm their land and then turn themselves into sea pirates, etc. Look for examples of people who have to struggle for existence today – against the elements, in war-torn areas, etc.

Knowledge and skills
People have bettered their lot by developing new skills and knowledge. This is reflected in the growth of inventions through the ages

– the wheel, bricks, hot-air balloons, electricity, etc. Look at some inventions in use around us and how they affect our lives today.

Civilisation

As people developed they began to gather together, first in communities and then whole civilisations – the Babylonians, the Egyptians, the Greeks, the Romans, etc. Examine some of these civilisations – how they were the same and how they were different.

National Curriculum geography

This year the teacher will continue to help her children study areas at home and overseas. In particular she will encourage them to:

- examine, describe and compare different areas;
- increase their knowledge of the physical aspects of the environment.

There are a number of geographical concepts which could help your child understand the basic aspects of the curriculum. Show her examples of these ideas locally and encourage her to see how these same ideas may be used in a wider context.

Change and continuity

From the beginning of people's time on Earth they have tried to change their surroundings and locality when they thought that it was advisable to do this, for example, when crops ran out, when the climate proved unsuitable, etc. At the same time, people have always tried to keep what they thought was useful to them, knowledge of cooking, building, etc. and to continue these helpful parts of their lives when they have moved. Ask your child to look at her own neighbourhood. What things have changed in the area? What other things need changing? What things should be kept? Why?

Location

People have always paid a great deal of attention to the areas in which they settled. They usually chose their locations because

YEAR 4 – AGES EIGHT TO NINE

they provided good areas in which to settle and live. Help your child to talk about her own area. What geographical features are there – hills, valleys, sources of water, etc.? What are the houses like? What forms of transport are there? What do the shops sell?

National Curriculum art

Over the year the teacher will help the children to:

- express their feelings and experiences in different forms of art, showing an increasing mastery of techniques and materials;
- begin to recognise that works of art are affected by the intentions of the artists creating them.

At home, continue to give your child as much practice as possible with different techniques and materials. Over the year you could encourage her to create works of art out of recycled materials, using as many different tools and materials as possible. Here are a few examples she might try:

Egg-box holders
See how many objects she can make from egg-boxes. Make artificial flowers by cutting out the individual holders, cutting down their sides and spreading them out in the shape of flowers. Paint them and let them dry. Put a pipe-cleaner through the centre of each flower to form the stem.

Make a totem-pole out of an egg-box. First of all study pictures of totem poles, and then cut out the individual egg-holders. Glue them on top of one another, and then glue the whole assembly to a base. Finally, paint designs on the totem pole.

Use egg-boxes to make heads for puppets, or a sailing vessel – indeed, anything you can think of.

Robots

Make model robots out of tin cans and other junk such as collections of corks and pins, or wire and assorted nails. Think of other junk sculptures you could make.

Coats of arms

Look at pictures of coats of arms, and try making a model coat-of-arms from a tin lid. First flatten the tin lid with a hammer, and then scratch a simple design on both sides of the lid with a nail. Working from the inside of the tin lid, hammer a blunt nail around the scratched pattern in a stippling effect. This should force the shape of the design out of the other side of the tin. Now turn the lid over and paint the embossed design with varnish. Try using this technique to make other patterns.

(**NB** Adult supervision will be needed with this activity.)

National Curriculum music

Over the year the teacher will follow the National Curriculum by helping the children to:

- sing and play, improving their knowledge of performing music, so that they can transmit their musical ideas to others;
- listen to music appreciatively and begin to understand some aspects of the history of music.

Over the year you could help the teacher by improving your child's knowledge of musical instruments and their history. Let her see musical instruments being played at concerts or on the television, and encourage her to find out how they have developed over the years.

The first people made music by clapping, and striking wood and stones together. Ask your child to make her own musical instruments from objects around her. How many different sounds can she make from the same object? Make sounds from wooden spoons and bottles filled with different amounts of water and struck with a piece of metal. Try to arrange these different sounds into a piece of music.

YEAR 4 – AGES EIGHT TO NINE

National Curriculum physical education

Over this year the teacher will be helping the children to:

- develop their skills in games, gymnastics, dance, athletics, outdoor and adventurous activities and swimming;
- respond imaginatively to the physical challenges they encounter in these activities, working on their own and as members of a team.

Your child will be performing an increasingly complex set of educational gymnastics at school. You can reinforce the work of the teacher and help your child at home by concentrating on the three basic components of these movements – space, time and weight.

Help her to understand that any movement can go in a number of different ways, depending upon the amount of space available. Ask her to perform basic movements – running, hopping, jumping, etc. in different areas, so that she has to adjust her movements according to the space she has in which to perform them. Go on by asking her to perform the same movements at different speeds – quickly, slowly and speeds in between. Ask her to work out the differences in the movements depending upon the amount of time available in which to perform them. The third component, weight, means that movements vary depending upon the amount of weight put on them by your child. They may be performed heavily or lightly.

Over the course of the year ask your child to show you the different combinations of movements she can perform, and see that she performs them in different areas of space, time and weight. The movements could be performed slowly and lightly in a confined space, or quickly and heavily in plenty of space, or quickly and lightly in a confined space, or in any other combination. The mixture of these three elements will decide how a movement is performed and will give the movement its quality.

Problems

 Now that my child is in Year 4 I find that she does not want to work at home with me nearly as much as she did earlier in the school. Is there anything I can do about this?

Your child will be doing so much at school this year that she will not want to do as much at home as she used to. However, she will still be looking to you for support. This year do not attempt to have organised National Curriculum sessions at home during term-time, unless she asks for them. Instead, put aside half an hour a day during the holidays. You will be surprised at the advances your child is making, and even in the holidays all that you really need to do is revise the work she is doing at school. This is still a very important and useful function. You will probably find that over the next two years there will be more opportunities for helping with the National Curriculum at home.

End of Year 4 checklists

Most, but not all children should be able to meet the majority of these targets by the end of Year 4. They should also, of course, still be able to meet the requirements set for the previous years.

English

Speaking and listening
The child:

- can contribute usefully to a discussion;
- can follow the line of an argument and respond to it;
- can cope with sudden changes in a conversation.

Reading
The child:

- can read for enjoyment and discuss intelligently what has been read;

- can find a word in a dictionary;
- can find a subject in an encyclopaedia.

Writing

The child:

- can write simple stories;
- can write descriptions;
- can pick out the important points in a situation and write about them;
- is willing to try new forms of creative writing suggested by a parent or teacher.

Grammar

The child:

- is beginning to understand the meaning of verbs and nouns;
- is beginning to understand when to use *a* and *an* before a noun.

Handwriting

The child is beginning to form a distinctive, clear form of joined handwriting.

Spelling

The child is beginning to spell with increasing confidence and to use a dictionary to find how to spell words.

Mathematics

Number

The child:

- is showing an increasing grasp of tables;
- understands and can use table squares;
- is beginning to work with fractions and decimals;
- can add, subtract, divide and multiply tens and units;
- can work out simple mathematical problems;
- is beginning to use standard measures of weight, capacity and length;

- is beginning to add, subtract, multiply and divide units of money, time, weight, length and capacity.

Shape, space and measures
The child is beginning to find areas by counting squares.

Handling data
The child:

- is using timetables and calendars;
- can solve simple crossword and jigsaw puzzles.

Science

Life processes and living things
The child understands the importance of food and its nutritional value.

Materials and their properties
The child understands what physical and chemical changes are.

Physical processes
The child is beginning to conduct experiments to understand what light is and how we see things.

Design and technology

Designing skills
The child is beginning to use a variety of sources to help her plan her work – plans, videos, observation, etc.

Making skills
The child is showing an increasing confidence in her selection and use of materials, tools and techniques.

History

The child:

- is showing an increasing awareness that history is divided into periods of time – civilisations, etc.;

- is beginning to learn more about different civilisations;
- is showing an increasing awareness of how things have changed and developed over the centuries.

Geography

The child:

- can understand that people seek to change some aspects of their environment and keep others as they are;
- knows that people select certain physical conditions in which to live – shelter, water, suitable climate, etc.

Art

Investigating and making
The child:

- is selecting relevant resources and materials;
- is beginning to think about and, where necessary, change her work.

Knowledge and understanding
The child is studying and comparing the work of artists.

Music

Performing and composing
The child:

- is beginning to rehearse and present her own musical projects;
- is beginning to compose music of her own.

Listening and appraising
The child can identify sounds made by different musical instruments.

Physical education

The child:

- is enjoying aspects of dance, gymnastics, outdoor and adventurous activities, athletics and swimming;
- can perform simple feats of agility – forward rolls, backward rolls, bridges, cartwheels, etc.

Parents talking

When I was a kid my parents used to send me to Sunday School every Sunday and Brownies during the week, so that they could get a bit of peace and quiet now and again. Now that I've got children of my own all the emphasis seems to be on helping them at home. I reckon I was born out of my time. Whatever happened to the good old days?

The headmaster seems to think that helping our kids at home with the National Curriculum is developing a new breed of super-parents able to check up on him. He keeps on going around correcting the spellings on the notices on the staffroom wall.

Useful books for eight- to nine-year-olds

English (Reading books)

The Glory Gardens series, Bob Cattell (Julia MacRae)
Katie Morag series, Mairi Hedderwick (Bodley Head)
Herculeah Jones series, Betsy Byars (Bodley Head)
Orson Cart series, Steve Donald (Hutchinson)
The Oxford Book of Scarytales, Dennis Pepper (OUP)

YEAR 4 – AGES EIGHT TO NINE

Mathematics

Investigating Maths, Robert Fisher and Alan Vince (Simon and Schuster)
Simple Maths, Rose Griffiths (A and C Black)

Science

Megabugs, Miranda MacQuitty and Laurence Mound (Riverswift)
Science Questions and Answers (*Earth Science*, *Plant Science*, etc.), Anita Ganeri (Evans)

Design and Technology

Make it Work (*Mills and Big Wheels*, etc.), Peter Firmin (A and C Black)
Built With a Purpose (*Railways*, *Windmills*, etc.), Althea and Edward Parker (A and C Black)

History

I Was There series (*First World War*, *Industrial Revolution*, etc.), John D. Clare (ed.) (Riverswift)

Geography

Wildlifers series (*African Elephant*, *Giant Panda*, etc.), Melissa Kim (Hutchinson)

Art

The Junior Art Pack, Ron Van Der Meer (Cape)

Music

Sonsense Nongs, Michael Rosen (A and C Black)

CHAPTER SEVEN

Year 5 – Ages nine to ten

❝ *As a young teacher, after months of argument, I finally persuaded my headmistress to let me send some paper and pencils home from school for the children to work on the National Curriculum with their parents. She had a strong sense of thrift and it was with enormous reluctance that finally she blew the dust off the store-room lock and opened it for me. I felt like Ali Baba after he had learnt the meaning of the words "Open Sesame!"* ❞

By this year most children have got their heads down and are getting on nicely. They have been with their peers for three or four years and usually have their place firmly established in the social structure of the class, with friends and alliances worked out. They know what they are doing, and while they may lack the spontaneity and eagerness to impress, so apparent in Year 4, as a rule they are perfectly happy to work, as long as they have confidence in the adults who are helping them.

Often this is a year in which children turn increasingly to their parents for help with their school work. This is not always because they are anxious to establish a fresh rapport, but probably has more to do with the fact that they are learning so much at school that they realise that they need all the help they can get and that, on a good day, parents can be a surprisingly effective form of support.

Do not be surprised therefore if, over this year, your child's vocabulary is extended quite often to the use of the muttered request, 'Give us a hand with this, will you?' Even if the wish is not put into words, you will find that your child is now quite receptive to offers of help at home.

National Curriculum English

Children will be expected to:

- talk and listen with confidence, paying attention to the ideas and values of others;
- understand ideas, events and characters in the books they read, discussing these and giving examples from the stories to back up their statements, and search for information in books;
- write in more detail in many different ways, developing ideas and presenting arguments. Sentences should be longer and grammatical in joined, legible handwriting.

Helping with reading, speaking and listening

With all the work which has been done at school and at home your child should now be reading fairly fluently and be prepared to look at different forms of reading matter. Try to persuade him to continue reading books for pleasure and information, but do not worry too much if this proves to be a bit of a battle at this stage. Very often, now that he has mastered the rudiments of reading he will want to use his skills on what he regards as more 'grown-up' forms of writing rather than story books.

Working on the principle of 'if you can't beat 'em, join 'em', give your child chances to read newspapers, magazines, brochures and instructional manuals. Comics do not have the same hold on children as they once did. Boys and girls seem to leap from reading simple books to studying newspapers and other everyday forms of written material, leaving out the comic stage altogether, just as they make the transition from watching schools' television programmes to adult programmes, showing little interest in the programmes intended for children.

At this stage it is important that you keep your child reading by hook or by crook, so that he does not drift away from the habit altogether. It will be a real bonus if he is still building up his own collection of favourite books and authors – and some children will do this for the rest of their lives. However, if yours is one of the majority of children who does not spend much time with books at this age, then encourage him to read the newspaper or magazines, and ask his opinion of what he has read, trying to ensure, as tactfully as possible, that he gives comprehensive and thoughtful answers. Try him on the following activities.

Weather forecasts
Check on the efficiency of weather forecasts in a newspaper. Cut out the weather forecasts for a number of days and stick them in a small notebook, leaving a blank page opposite each forecast. In due time, write down what the actual weather was like for the day of the forecast. Check the number of times that the forecast was right.

Football results
Read the sports pages to see what the experts say about the chances of favourite football matches. Later, read the accounts of the actual matches. How close were the experts to forecasting what actually happened?

Travel brochures
Read travel brochures about the place you are going to for your annual holiday. Later, discuss how accurate the brochures were compared with the reality of the holiday.

Free offers
Collect pamphlets from supermarkets and stores which contain 'free offers' of goods. Read them and discuss them. How many seem worthwhile and how many look useless? Enter some of the word competitions on the backs of the pamphlets.

Writing

By now the teacher will probably be spending some time on helping her children to present their written work in an acceptable and attractive form. This is an important part of language development. Its importance is reflected in the fact that considerable attention is paid to it in the tests taken next year at Key Stage 2.

At home, encourage your child to begin writing stories, accounts of activities, reports, etc. You can really help the school this year by making sure that each piece of writing undertaken by your child goes through the following stages:

Planning: Make notes about the first ideas for a piece of writing, just to get something down upon which to build.

Drafting: Start writing a rough outline of the piece of work, putting it into some sort of order, with a recognisable beginning, middle and end.

Revising: Work on the draft, improving and polishing it, until the piece of writing is completed.

Proof-reading: Go through the draft, making sure that the writing is organised and sensible, checking the spelling and punctuation.

Presenting: Prepare the final copy which should be neat, well written and as free from errors as possible.

Try to make sure that this order of events becomes almost second nature to your child whenever he writes something.

Children of this age often enjoy writing poetry, because it gives them a chance to experiment with words and does not take up too much of their time. Give your child a chance to write limericks and short poems, and introduce him to other forms of verse.

Haiku

Write a *haiku*, a Japanese poem of three lines designed to paint a picture of a scene in words. The first and third line of a haiku both have five syllables, while the second line has seven syllables:

> *A bird on a branch*
> *Sings sweetly all through the day*
> *Drowned by the traffic*
>
> *The girl won the race,*
> *Falling through the hand-held tape,*
> *Too tired to stand up.*

The mechanics of writing

The teacher will revise the basic use of full stops, capital letters and commas. She will go over the meanings of nouns and verbs, singular and plural. She will probably introduce the children to the use of adjectives.

Most efforts suggesting that children study nouns and adjectives at home will not be well received by the majority of children of this age. However, if you can stimulate your child's interest in words and their uses by the use of a few simple activities it will certainly supplement the work being done at school.

Proper nouns

Look through the local telephone directory to see how many people have the names of jobs – Baker, Smith, Butcher, etc. – or places – Lancaster, York, etc. Look through the directory and see if you can guess the origins of any other names in it.

Adjectives

Write down a list of suitable adjectives for an animal. For a snake one could use adjectives such as: long, twisting, cold, venomous, deadly, fast, coiled, hooded, cold-blooded, etc. Then write these adjectives down in such a way that they form the shape of the animal being described.

Spelling

Encourage your child to keep an illustrated dictionary of his hobby or favourite sport, cutting out pictures from newspapers and magazines to accompany the words and their meanings.

National Curriculum mathematics

This year the teacher will be teaching her children to:

- seek out and use any information necessary for solving mathematical problems;
- use simple fractions and percentages, add and subtract decimals;
- use a variety of measuring instruments to explore the sizes of areas;
- begin to study problems, using mathematical information and data, working out whether certain results are 'certain', 'likely', or 'unlikely'.

This year the teacher, in addition to introducing new aspects of the mathematics curriculum, will continue to revise the skills and techniques acquired by the children over the past few years. She will concentrate on the four rules – addition, subtraction, division and multiplication. She will expect the children to be able to apply these four rules to thousands, hundreds, tens and units, to length (kilometres, metres, centimetres), to weight (kilogrammes and grammes), to capacity (litres) and to money (pounds and pence).

You can help at home by encouraging your child to think logically, by playing board games such as chess and draughts, and to grow accustomed to using numbers, by playing dominoes.

Whenever possible use the terms *total*, *product* and *difference* as you talk about figures with your child. The total is what we get as a result of adding numbers, the product is the result of multiplying numbers, and we get the difference if we subtract numbers from one another.

Show him the importance of money in everyday life by showing him bills and receipts as you receive them, and talk about these. Show him how you write cheques and adjust the balance after you have spent money. Go through catalogues together, discussing the prices of the goods advertised. Compare the prices of the same goods in different catalogues and advertisements.

You can reinforce the work being done at school on fractions and percentages by casually introducing these into your activities together – 'I've painted about a quarter of that wall,' 'There's about ten per cent of that jar still to be filled,' etc.

Help your child appreciate the importance of gathering and using data by looking at various dials around the house – temperatures shown on stoves, different clock faces, and so on.

Equipment

Your child will be using different types of mathematical equipment at school. Make sure that he knows how to handle the different tools.

Protractor: Help your child to measure the angles of triangles with a protractor. Take it in turns to measure and then check the angles. See if he can draw his own lines at a simple angle of, say, 90 and 45 degrees.

Compasses: Use a set of compasses to draw circles of different shapes, by adjusting the compasses.

Stop-watch: Time simple activities around the house – boiling an egg, cooking something in a microwave, etc.

Areas

Work out the areas of surfaces by placing small square counters inside each surface and counting them. This can only be a rough measurement, because there will usually be some space left over. Experiment with placing the squares to leave as little space as possible.

Probability

Probability is an aspect of mathematics in which the child is asked to use reason to work out the chances of something happening.

Play a series of games with your child in which he is asked to say whether a thing is *certain to happen, may happen,* or *probably will not happen.* Start by dropping a number of objects into a bowl or basin of water. Use objects made of many different materials – metal, plastic, wood, paper, etc. Ask your child to forecast whether each object is certain to sink, may sink, or probably will not sink. Keep a record to see how many times he made the correct forecast.

Repeat this activity in a number of different contexts – which objects will fall straight to the ground when dropped from a height, and which may flutter more slowly down, etc.

Shapes

Engage in practical work with shapes by making a number of different *pyramid* shapes. These are shapes which start from a broad base and taper towards the top. Use the same materials on different-sized bases, and then use different materials. Compare and contrast the different pyramids made.

National Curriculum science

This term the teacher will be trying to help the children to:

- carry out more scientific investigations, deciding what to measure, how to measure it and what equipment to use;

- use the results of their investigations to decide upon general scientific principles, for example, food left exposed will grow bacteria which can harm that food.
- devise tests to back up these principles, for example, leave some milk exposed to the sun and air and put another similar sample of milk in a refrigerator. The milk left exposed should go bad first.
- continue to develop knowledge in the general areas of science known as 'materials and their properties', 'life processes and living things', and 'physical processes'.

This year the teacher will be encouraging the children to use their powers of reasoning to proceed from the known to the unknown in science. She will also be helping them to devise fair tests in order to prove different scientific principles. You can help at home by stimulating your child to carry out a number of scientific tests and experiments which will supplement and make sense of some of the work she is doing at school. Here are some ideas:

Life and living processes – breathing

Test your lung power by inflating your lungs and exhaling through a rubber tube into a bowl of water. How long is it before bubbles stop appearing because your lungs are now empty and you have to breathe in again? Make a note of the time it takes to exhale – this will show your lung power.

Compare your lung power with that of other people in the house.

Would it be a fair test to compare your lung power with that of a grown-up?

Would it be a fair test to compare your lung power with that of other children of roughly your age and size?

Do all animals breathe? Why is it important?

Do all animals breathe in through their lungs, or do some animals use another method?

Life and living processes – beaks

Over a period of several months make a study of different birds in the garden. Look at their beaks. Are they all the same shape?

Make drawings of the different beaks you see. Look at photographs and drawings of birds in information books. Find a picture of a heron. Its beak is long and thin to allow it to spear a fish and hold it. Now find a picture of a finch. Its beak is short and powerful to allow it to break open seeds.

Look at the drawings of beaks you have made and guess what each beak will be good at doing.

Put a bottle of milk with a foil top outside a window. See if a bird tries to open the top with its beak. Why do all birds need beaks?

Materials and their properties – tablets and salts

This is an activity to see how tablets work in our bodies, but you **must work with your child** on this experiment, as your child will be mixing chemicals with other things. This can be dangerous if you use the wrong chemicals.

Place an Alka Seltzer tablet in a glass of water. What happens to it? Why does this happen? What would happen to it if you swallowed this tablet?

Stir some health salts into a glass of water. What happens to the powder? Why does this happen?

Do not use any other pills or tablets for these experiments.

Materials and their properties – invisible ink

This is an activity to make some invisible ink by squeezing lemon juice from a lemon into a glass.

Dip a small paint-brush into the lemon juice. Write a message on a piece of paper, dipping the brush often into the juice.

Leave the message to dry. It should disappear.

Get an adult to place the paper in an oven set at a low temperature for about fifteen minutes.

After fifteen minutes ask the adult to take the paper out. The message should have reappeared. The juice has dried and disappeared from sight, but has been brought back by the heat of the oven.

Physical processes – magnetic sculptures

Collect a number of different magnets and use them to attract metal objects. Gather together a number of small pieces of metal and magnetise each in turn by stroking it repeatedly in the same direction along the bar of a powerful magnet. When each piece of metal has been magnetised the different pieces will stick together. Make a number of magnetised sculptures by sticking the metal pieces together.

National Curriculum design and technology

The teacher will be helping the children to:

- look critically at designs and man-made objects;
- develop ideas and organise plans of work;
- make and test an increasingly complex number of mechanisms;
- remake objects based on flaws observed in earlier attempts.

Continue to help your child to design and make everyday practical objects and to appreciate the craftsmanship in other manufactured articles. Involve him in trying to help you solve everyday problems about the house – how can something be kept warm and dry, how best can something be decorated, and so on. Here are some ideas:

Insulation

Examine efforts made in the house to retain heating – lagging pipes, etc. Now fill four identical tins with warm (not hot) water. Make sure that each tin has a removable top. Select four different types of insulation material – wool, cloth, paper, etc. and wrap the same amount of material around each tin. Experiment with different ways of shaping and wrapping the material to make it an effective insulator or retainer of heat.

Use a thermometer to take the temperature of the water in each tin at regular intervals. Which material helps to retain the heat the longest? Experiment with different shapes and materials for the water containers. Does the shape make any difference to retaining heat? Does the material make any difference?

Waterproofing

Make a collection of different materials – cotton, denim, nylon, rayon, etc. Work out tests for seeing which material is the most waterproof (sprinkle the material with water, etc.). Decide which material is the most waterproof, and from this material design and make a waterproof cloak for a doll. Test the cloak to see if it is *(a)* waterproof *(b)* quite waterproof *(c)* not waterproof at all.

Rugs and carpets

Examine the rugs and carpets in the house. Make a collection of other pieces of carpet. Look at the designs and material and compare them. Look at the undersides of the carpets. How have they been constructed so that they will not slide across the floor? Make a collection of many different materials and devise tests to see which of these materials would make the safest non-slip underside for a rug.

National Curriculum history

The teacher will select one or more of the periods of history suggested for study in the National Curriculum. In addition she will try to arouse in the child a general interest in history and an awareness of a number of historical areas:

- *change:* over a period of time some things have changed quite quickly while others have changed very little;

- *evidence:* unless we have evidence that something has happened it is very difficult to know what really happened in history;
- *sources:* we can often find this evidence in sources, like documents, eye-witness accounts, newspaper reports, etc. Some sources are more reliable than others.

As well as helping your child examine the period of history being taught at school, you can also give him a deeper and richer appreciation of the subject in a number of ways. Look for sources of history in your area – buildings, areas with stories attached to them, statues, etc. Look for buildings in the area which seem to have changed little over the years. How do you know that they are old? Can you tell from the shape or colour, or is it the design that makes them look old?

Origins

Children can often be encouraged to take an interest in history by investigating the origins of everyday objects and trying to find pictures of these objects at different periods, for example:

Homes: The first homes built by people were probably windbreaks made of branches and leaves stuck into the ground, behind which people could shelter.

Beds: These probably originated as piles of leaves and twigs and were gradually replaced by heaps of animal skins.

Pillows: The first pillows were probably small logs of wood.

Spades: These were developed from digging sticks, with sharpened points hardened in a fire.

Baskets: The first baskets were probably fashioned from pieces of bark.

Names

A number of words and phrases have entered our language based on the names of people who lived long ago. Here are just a few examples:

The phrase *'as strong as Samson'* is based on the exploits of the Old Testament strong man.

To *boycott*, meaning to have nothing to do with someone, is based on the Irish peasants who ignored the landowner, Captain Boycott.

The word *sandwich* is derived from Lord Sandwich who, rather than leave the gambling tables, had his food delivered in the shape of slices of meat between rounds of bread.

A *Bowie knife* is named after its American inventor Jim Bowie, who died at the siege of the Alamo.

Are there any names connected with history in your area? Are there names of roads, buildings, estates named after people? Who were these people?

National Curriculum geography

The teacher will continue to try to arouse the interest of her children in life at home and overseas, the weather and the environment. In particular she will expect the children to begin to develop a knowledge of:

- the local environment and other areas at home and overseas;
- the names and locations of some major cities at home and overseas;
- the names and locations of some countries in Europe;
- basic map-reading.

If you show your child how to work out a number of geographical ideas and principles in your own area this will help him with the more theoretical aspects of the subject he will be covering at school this year.

A subject in which most children of this age show a keen interest in food. If you use this interest as a springboard for a number of home activities a considerable part of the background of the curriculum will be covered in this way. Take, for instance, the topic of breakfast cereals. Ask your child to make a list of the different breakfast cereals in the house. How many are there? What are their names? What are the pictures like on the boxes? How are the cereals described on the boxes? Which is his favourite breakfast cereal? Why does he like it?

How is his particular favourite cereal made? How many cereals are made something like Cornflakes? Where do the ingredients come from? (Cornflakes are made by mixing small pieces of corn with sugar, salt and a malt extract made from barley. The grains are cooked, softened and then partly dried in ovens. They are rolled into thin flakes and toasted until they are crisp. Vitamins are added and the flakes are packed into boxes.)

How many cereals can he find in a shop or supermarket which are made like Shredded Wheat? Where do the ingredients come from? (Shredded Wheat is made from grains of wheat. The wheat is washed and cooked in boiling water. It is left to dry, rolled into shapes, made crisp in an oven and packed.)

How many cereals can he find in a shop or supermarket which are made like Weetabix? Where do the ingredients come from? (Weetabix is made by mixing wheat with malt extract from barley, sugar and salt. The mixture is cooked in pressure cookers until the wheat has soaked up the liquid. When the mixture is soft it is rolled into flakes and the flakes are pressed into biscuit shapes and baked in an oven.)

National Curriculum art

Over the year the teacher will help her children to:

- show a command of different techniques and materials by choosing and using appropriate means to depict objects and feelings;
- show an understanding of other cultures by looking at the ways they depict objects and feelings;
- make use of comparisons with the work of well-known artists to improve their own work.

You can help the teacher considerably this year by showing your child examples of art and architecture in the locality and encouraging him to use the techniques he is developing by making his own artistic representations of what he has seen and felt.

Scraper pictures

Visit a local building with an attractive ceiling or wall. Ask your child how he thinks the artist or builder achieved his effects. Get him to try to make his own version of the ceiling or wall, using a scraper picture.

To make a scraper board, take a piece of white card and cover it with wax by rubbing two light-coloured crayons over it. Cover the wax with Indian ink. When the ink has dried scrape on your version of the wall or ceiling, using a sharp tool.

Stained glass

Visit a local church and study the stained-glass windows. Get your child to design and make his own version of a stained-glass window. This is what he needs to do:
Find a glass jar and draw your design or picture on a piece of paper the same size as the side of the jar. Place the drawing inside the jar, pressed against the side so that the picture shows through the side. Use outlining black to go over the outline of the picture on the outside of the jar, and when the outline is dry use transparent glass-painting colours to decorate the picture.

Stick-printing logo

Look at a number of logos used by large companies in the area. A logo is an attractively designed sign used to represent a company. It is used on the company's letters, in advertisements and on notice boards. Get your son to design and make his own logo for a local company using stick-printing. Help your child to cut shapes into the ends of a number of small sticks. Use squares, triangles, circles, etc. for the shapes. Soak a number of pads with different coloured paints and then put the ends of the sticks into the pads and transfer the shapes on to paper to make a logo.

National Curriculum music

Over this year the teacher will be revising all the musical skills taught over the previous years, and also helping children to:

- develop fresh musical skills in order to listen to and sing back longer musical phrases;
- learn the correct playing techniques for different percussion instruments – drums, etc.;
- listen to music from a wide variety of periods – nineteenth century, eighteenth century etc. – and styles – folk, jazz, opera, etc.

Help your child at home by giving him as many opportunities as possible to listen to different kinds of music. If you are particularly interested in one kind of music yourself, talk about it to him and try to convey your enthusiasm. Encourage him to listen to different percussion instruments and try to show him how these instruments can produce a strong rhythm for movement and dancing.

Stamping sticks

One of the first percussion instruments was the *stamping stick*, used in the South Pacific. This consists of a hollow stick with one end sealed. The sealed end is beaten against the ground, which makes the sound come up the empty tube, creating a distinct echo. Ask your child to design and make his own stamping stick, with one end sealed. Let him experiment with it by beating it against different surfaces to see which gives the most effective sound. Help him to devise and practise different rhythms with the stick.

National Curriculum physical education

Over this year the teacher will be helping the children to:

- be able to memorise and repeat a series of movements, such as a dance or gymnastics sequence;
- evaluate these performances;

- adapt a movement or dance to the mood of a piece of music;
- understand the importance of warming-up properly before taking part in any physical activities.

You can help your child by giving him chances to supplement the outdoor and adventurous activities strand of the physical education curriculum. This is the area in which children have to use their common sense and physical dexterity to cope with different challenges in the environment. If your child can be persuaded to engage in one or two of these challenges each term it will help him to think and react to problems in a logical manner.

Traffic

Help your child to carry out a survey of traffic passing the house. How many vehicles pass the house in the course of an hour? What sorts of vehicles are they? Use his knowledge of local traffic, get him to draw a map showing the safest route to cycle to school.

Suggest that he makes a chart showing all the traffic signs and signals near your home. Should there be any more helpful signs erected? Why are they needed?

Play a game where you take it in turns to use a compass to follow sets of directions, for example, walk ten metres north, three metres west, two metres south, and so on.

(This will also link with geography activities.)

End of Year 5 checklists

Most, but not all children should be able to meet the majority of these targets by the end of Year 5. They should also still be able to meet the requirements set for previous years.

English

Speaking and listening
The child:

- can talk fluently to different audiences and individuals, adapting approaches to the abilities of the listeners;

- can listen and respond sympathetically and with understanding to different speakers.

Reading
The child:

- is still reading books for interest and information;
- can appreciate the importance and purposes of an increasing variety of reading material – newspapers, magazines, brochures, etc.

Writing
The child:

- is producing different kinds of writing to meet different needs;
- is now organising written work carefully – planning, drafting, revising, proof-reading and presenting a final draft.

Grammar
The child is beginning to use adjectives.

Handwriting
The child is producing a distinctive and legible form of writing.

Spelling
The child:

- has the confidence to make an effort to spell unfamiliar words;
- is using dictionaries to help.

Mathematics

Number
The child:

- can apply the four rules of addition, subtraction, multiplication and division to thousands, hundreds, tens and units; money, capacity, weight, length and time;
- understands the meaning of such mathematical terms as *total*, *product* and *difference*;

- is using fractions and percentages with increasing confidence.

Shape, space and measures
The child is working with an increasing variety of shapes, like *pyramids*.

Handling data
The child:

- is using more tools and instruments like *protractors*, *compasses* and *stopwatches*;
- is beginning to use the concept of *probability*, based on the use of data.

Science

Life processes and living things
The child understands the importance of breathing and how living things breathe.

Materials and their properties
The child understands that chemicals can be used to combat disease and improve health.

Physical processes
The child can devise and conduct experiments to show that he understands the principles of physical processes like magnetism.

Design and technology

The child is beginning to relate the strands of design and technology – *designing* and *making* – to everyday problems such as retaining heat, water-proofing, designing household decorations, etc.

History

The child is continuing to relate history to his own background by showing an interest in the origins of everyday things – buildings, names, words, etc.

Geography

The child is beginning to appreciate that the principles of geography can be helpful in understanding aspects of everyday life – food, homes, transport, etc.

Art

The child is investigating examples of art in the world around him, and using these examples to inspire his own work.

Music

The child is listening to different types of music, and is using this music to influence his own music-making.

Physical education

The child is taking an interest in movement and is using his increasing self-confidence to solve physical problems in games, dance and everyday life.

Parents talking

❛ *In one last desperate effort to get my son to read I put him in charge of all the junk mail that came through the letter-box, sorting it out and telling me what the letters were about. I had forgotten how easily influenced children of nine are. Now he's always trying to persuade me to buy the wretched stuff advertised in the junk mail. It's like having a persistent and very irritating door-to-door salesman living permanently in the house.* ❜

Useful books for nine- to ten-year-olds

English

Fun With English – Good Writing, William Edmonds (Chambers)
Evans Folk Tales, Sheila Hatherley (Evans)
Wordpower, Helen McLullich (Longman)

Mathematics

Maths 2: age 9–10, Sandra Soper (Pan Macmillan)
Calculator Practice: Age 9–10, Alan Brighouse, David Godber and Peter Patilla (Pan Macmillan)

Science

100 More Simple Science Experiments, Barbara Taylor (Kingfisher)
How Green Are You? David Bellamy (Frances Lincoln)

Design and Technology

The Wonderful World of Colour series (*Colour in Art and Advertising, Colour in Fashion and Costume*, etc.), Sally and Adrian Morgan (Evans)
Krazy Kites, David Pelham (Pan Macmillan)

History

I Wonder Why . . . series (*Pyramids Were Built, Castles Had Moats*, etc.), Philip Steele (Kingfisher)

Geography

Dictionary of British Place Names, Andrew Currie (Tiger Books)
Wild World of Animals series (*Deserts, Forests*, etc.), Michael Chinery (ed.) (Kingfisher)
The Travellers' Quiz Book, Deborah Manley (Pan Macmillan)

Music

Lively Music 9–11, Wendy Hart (Heinemann)

CHAPTER EIGHT

Year 6 – Ages ten to eleven

❝ As a headteacher I am all for parents helping with the National Curriculum. However, some of them get the bit between their teeth and want to expand their participation in school events a bit too much. Whenever I meet a new parent I have just one criterion. I ask myself, "Is this the sort of person who, one day, will try to persuade me to do a ten kilometres sponsored walk in aid of the School Fund?" ❞

Year 6, the final year of your child's primary school career, will arrive all too soon and it will be time for much stock-taking. What has your child achieved over the previous six years and how will this final year prepare her for the secondary education to come? Has she been happy? Has she developed as a person and grown into a self-confident, hard-working child, able to work both on her own and as a member of a team? The social side of school life is very important. The curriculum work being undertaken is, of course, very important as well.

For too long many parents have been denied the opportunity to see just how well their children are doing in the different subjects of the curriculum. The introduction of the National Curriculum and the assessment tests in the core subjects taken by all children in state schools means that we can now all judge for ourselves how our children are performing against the national standards.

Teaching and learning in Year 6

The introduction of the tests at age eleven does not mean that all teaching stops in Year 6 while the children are prepared for the tests. Far from it. This is one of the busiest of all school years, but it is busy in a different sense to most other periods in the primary school.

So far in the school your child will have been taught according to the levels laid down by the National Curriculum. By Year 6, however, the children in the class will have developed at vastly different rates. Many of them will have reached what is termed an average standard of achievement, a few will be lagging behind and will need a great deal of help in order to bring them up to the standard of the majority, while some will be shooting ahead and achieving levels more usually associated with children of twelve, thirteen and even fourteen years of age. This means that in Year 6 the teacher will be doing a great deal of small group and even individual teaching, so that each child in the class receives the type of education she or he needs at this time.

Because of this it may sometimes seem that the year as a whole is not making the same overall progress as in earlier years. They are, but it is a different type of progress. Individual strengths and weaknesses are being catered to. The teacher is working hard with each child as an individual, and not always with the class as a whole.

Key Stage 2 Assessment Tests

At first, the name of the game will be assessment. The teacher has to discover the level of attainment reached by each child in the different school subjects, and pinpoint strengths and weaknesses, so that she can prepare and deliver individual itineraries.

The teacher will be using the overall school work done by the children and individual tests she has devised in order to see just where each boy and girl in the class stands and what work is needed to improve his or her standard.

In May she will have further confirmation of the standards being attained, when the children take the National Assessment Tests in English, mathematics and science. The grades reached by the children in these subjects will be communicated in writing to the parents, and the class teacher or headteacher, or both, will arrange to discuss these results with parents in confidence.

The overall standards reached by the Year 6 children in these tests are usually produced in the annual report of the governors to parents, together with the overall standards reached by the primary schools under the jurisdiction of the local education authority. No individual results are given. Schools must send home written reports on the progress of children in all the National Curriculum subjects, not just the core ones, each year.

Levels

The Standard Assessment Tests at Key Stage 2 in English, mathematics and science are graded at different levels. An average child of eleven is expected to attain Level 4. Some may reach only the lower levels – 1, 2 and 3, while others will go on to reach the higher levels of 5 and 6. Level 6 is the average grade expected to be reached by fourteen-year-old children.

Sample tests – Key Stage 2

The sample tests given in this chapter, as in Chapter 4, are not intended to be exact duplicates of the ones your child will take in Year 6. However, they do cover the Key Stage 2 curriculum, have been used in a number of primary schools, and should give you some idea of the stage or level your child has reached at the time that she takes them.

The tests are designed in a progressive manner, starting with simple activities which should be within the scope of children capable of covering Level 3, and going on to Level 5.

As mentioned in Chapter 4, the size of this book prevents us from reproducing the tests in the same size and format as the 'real thing'. However, if possible, perhaps by getting your child to write down her answers on a separate sheet, let her attempt all the questions, but do not ask her to spend any time on questions she cannot answer. There is no time limit to the tests given in this chapter. Allow your child to work through them at her own pace. The answers are given at the end of the chapter. If you want to, at this stage you can work through each paper with your child. Do not help her with the answers, but discuss the questions with her and see how she approaches each one.

English tests

Children will be tested in their abilities at reading, writing, spelling and handwriting. A typical range of questions is shown below. No handwriting test has been set, but you can judge your child's progress here by looking at the handwriting used in the other answers. Look for a legible, distinctive style of joined handwriting.

Spelling

Copy the following stories, leaving the blanks with just the one letter in front of each one. Let your child have the copy with the blanks. Read the stories to your child but read out the whole word where there are blanks in your child's copy. Ask your child to fill in each blank with the correct spelling of the words. (The words are among the answers at the end of this chapter.)

Level 3

Snow

The snow lay on the g............. Its colour
was w............. The children saw the small
snow f............. drifting down from the
sky. They wore gloves because it was very
c............. They decided to build a
s............. They used stones for his eyes
and m............. They put an old hat on his
h............. When they had finished they
piled up snow in their hands and threw
s............. at it. After a time they got very
t............. and they all went h.............

Level 4

The Fox and the Grapes

A fox went to look for something to eat
because he was h............. He walked for a
long t............. He could not see any
f............. to eat anywhere. He t.............
that he would go where some grapes were
being g............. on vines. When he got to
the vines he l............. up. The grapes
were too h............. above his head. The
fox could not r............. them. This made
the fox very a............. "Ah well, I didn't
r............. want the grapes anyway," he
said.

Level 5

The Trojan Horse

The Greeks lay siege to the city of Troy for
ten years. Both sides f............. bravely.
The Greeks tried to a............. the walls of
Troy but could not d............. the walls.
The people of Troy were safe b.............
the walls. In the end the Greeks s.............
away in their ships. They left behind a
large wooden horse. It was mounted on
large, round w............. The people of
Troy d............. the horse into their city.
They did not know that there were Greek
s............. hidden inside the horse. When
it grew dark that n............. the men came
out of the horse and c............. the city.

One mark for each correct answer
Total: 30
Level 3: 1–10
Level 4: 11–20
Level 5: 21–30

Reading

Level 3

The Little Match Girl
(Hans Andersen)

A little match girl stood shivering in the
streets, trying to sell her boxes of
matches. The night was very cold and no
one would buy. In order to keep warm the

girl lit one of her matches. The brief flame warmed her. She dreamt for a moment of a wonderful Christmas tree covered with lights. Then she lit a second match and thought that she saw her beloved grandmother. One by one the girl struck all the matches. The next day her dead body was found huddled among the snowdrifts.

1 What was the girl selling?....................

2 Had she sold any? ....

3 What time was it? ....

4 What did she do to keep warm?...........

5 What did she think she saw? ....

6 What was the second thing she thought she saw?................................

7 How many matches did she strike?
....

8 What happened to her during the night? ....

9 Where was her body found? ....

10 Think of another title for the story
....

Level 4
If You Should Meet a Crocodile

If you should meet a crocodile,
Don't take a stick and poke him;
Ignore the welcome in his smile,
Be careful not to stroke him.
For as he sleeps upon the Nile,
He thinner gets and thinner;
And whene'er you meet a crocodile
He's ready for his dinner.

11 What animal is the story about?

....

12 What shouldn't you do to him?

....

13 What else shouldn't you do to him?

....

14 Where does he sleep? ....

15 What is the Nile? ....

16 What does he do as he sleeps?

....

17 What is he ready for? ....

18 Why is he ready for it? ....

19 Do you think this poem is serious or
amusing? ....

20 What does *ignore* mean? ....

Level 5

Telephone Directory

Name	Address	Telephone number
Bird, John	14, Cherry Walk	78934
Black, Mary	17, Grimsby Rd	79234
Blanding, Peter	26, Town Street	54670
Borrill, Emma	6, Church Lane	34587
Bowers, David	9, Bridge Avenue	56812
Brayford, Tim	12, Barnby Close	43256

21 Where does David Bowers live?............

22 What is the telephone number of Emma Borrill? ....

23 Who lives in Town Street? ....

24 Whose telephone number is 43256?
....

25 Where does Peter Blanding live?
....

26 Where does John Bird live?.................

27 Who lives in Grimsby Road?...............

28 Whose house has the number 14 on it?
....

29 Who lives in Barnby Close?................

30 What order are the names of the people in?...

One mark for each correct answer
Total: 30
Level 3: 1–10
Level 4: 11–20
Level 5: 21–30

Writing

It is difficult for parents to assess the writing capabilities of their children at Key Stage 2, because marking the children's efforts has become a highly specialised art, relying to a great extent on the teacher being able to compare your child's work with that of her peers. Children will be asked to write a short story, preparing a preliminary draft, showing that they are capable of creating a plot, making up interesting and effective beginnings and endings to stories, developing characters and dialogue and creating interest among the readers. Sometimes there is an alternative to writing a story, with the child being given the option of writing a letter or a description of something.

Mathematics tests

Level 1

1
56	73	49	36	79
+	+	+	+	+
12	23	32	15	18

2
123	345	456	876	509
−	−	−	−	−
45	17	80	458	16

3 *Missing numbers:* Put in the missing number where there is an '*x*' in each sum below:

```
456          6xx
1xx +        431 +
599         1103
```

4 What is the time shown on each of these clocks?

YEAR 6 – AGES TEN TO ELEVEN

5 What temperatures are these thermometers showing?

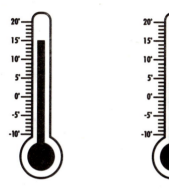

Level 4

6 *Factors:* The factors of a number are those numbers that divide exactly into that number. Write down all the factors of 30.

7 Write down the *difference* between these sets of numbers:
(a) 895 436 *(b)* 987 123 *(c)* 459 321

8 8756 tins of fruit are stored in a warehouse. 456 tins are sent out to a supermarket. How many tins are left in the warehouse?

9 A number multiplied by 3 gives the answer 27. What is the number?

10 If a + 12 = 18, what number does *'a'* stand for?

11 If a clock says that the time is 8.05 a.m. but the clock is ten minutes fast, what time is it really?

12 What is a half of each of these numbers?

(a) 44   *(b)* 8   *(c)* 16   *(d)* 10   *(e)* 6

Level 5

13

16	36	45	29
×	×	×	×
9	8	7	6

14 For the first three football matches of the season the crowds were 10,567, 12,679 and 15,864. How many people attended the three matches altogether?

15 Find the *product* of these numbers:

(a) 654 and 3   *(b)* 896 and 2
(c) 567 and 9   *(d)* 456 and 12

16 A cricketer made these scores in four matches:

16   44   12   15

What was his *average* score?

17 *Decimals:* add 4.4 to each of these numbers:

(a) 16.3   *(b)* 24.5
(c) 12.4   *(d)* 234.6
(e) 136.8

18 *Temperatures:* What are the temperatures at these times:

(a) 6.00 a.m. *(b)* 7.00 a.m.
(c) 8.00 a.m. *(d)* 9.00 a.m.
(e) 10.00 a.m.

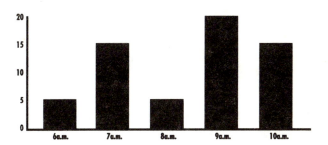

One mark for each correct answer
Total: 60
Level 3: 1–20
Level 4: 21–40
Level 5: 41–60

Science tests

Level 3

1 Why was marble used for the building of temples and palaces?

2 Why is slate used for the roofs of buildings?

3 How did ancient people turn clay into bricks?

4 What are these bridges called?

(a)

(b)

(c)

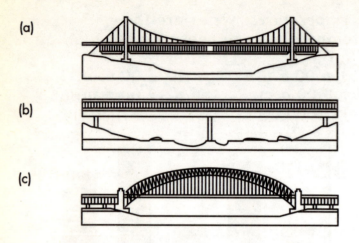

5 What gives us the four seasons?

6 Name four planets.

7 Where does the Moon get its light from?

8 Draw a diagram to show how a pendulum works.

9 What is the waste product breathed out of the lungs?

10 Carbon dioxide is one of the main gases found in air. What is the other?

11 Name the three main types of rock.

12 What is a fossil?

YEAR 6 – AGES TEN TO ELEVEN

Level 4

13 Name three materials from which birds build their nests in Britain.

14 What is the name given to the mass movements of birds when they fly away to warmer lands in the Winter?

15 What part of the bird's head can give us a clue as to the type of food it eats?

16 What is an *element*?

17 The heat of the Sun reaches us through its r............ Complete this word.

18 What is the process called when something solid disappears in water?

19 What do we call the process when water becomes ice?

20 Name five kinds of stone or rock.

21 What does a battery store?

22 When electricity moves from a battery through wires to light a bulb this is known as completing an electrical c............ Complete the word.

23 What is a *conductor* of electricity?

24 What will form on iron if it is left exposed to the elements?

25 What will happen if you focus the rays of the Sun through a magnifying glass on to a piece of paper?

26 What does the word *transparent* mean?

Level 5

27 Draw a diagram showing how the *water cycle* works. (Marks out of 5)

28 What is *water vapour*?

29 What is *energy*?

30 Sound is caused by v............. Complete the word.

31 What is it in our throats which move and allow us to talk?

32 What are *bacteria*?

33 How can bacteria harm people?

34 How can bacteria be helpful?

35 What word do we give to mushrooms and toadstools?

YEAR 6 – AGES TEN TO ELEVEN

36 What ingredient is used in the making of beer and wine and also makes bread rise or swell?

37 Name three different ways of preserving food, so that bacteria cannot harm it.

38 What is a *field of attraction* for a magnet?

39 What does the word *absorb* mean?

40 What does *weathering* mean?

One mark for each correct answer unless otherwise stated
Total: 60
Level 3: 1–20
Level 4: 21–40
Level 5: 41–60

Design and technology

Level 3

1 What is a *wheel*?

2 What is a *lever*?

3 What is a *ramp*?

4 What do you do if you *recycle* something?

5 What is a *puppet*?

6 What would you use a *screwdriver* for?

7 How do you make *papier-mâché?*

8 What do you do if you *assemble* something?

9 What do you do if you *solder* something?

10 What do you do if you *trace* something?

Level 4

11 What is a *sun-dial*?

12 What is *insulation*?

13 What do you do if you *design* something?

14 What are you doing if you are *pulping* something?

15 How would you make a model snake from string and cotton reels?

16 How would you make a telephone out of two empty cans and some string?

17 How would you make a *shaking* instrument?

18 How would you make a *pillar* out of a piece of paper and some adhesives?

19 How would you test the *strength* of this pillar?

20 Why are most roofs *sloping*?

Level 5
21 How would you make a bark rubbing?

22 How would you make a wind-sock?

23 How would you make a rain-gauge?

24 How would you make a pair of bellows from a squeezy bottle?

25 How would you test a number of carrier bags from different local stores to see which one was the strongest?

26 What could you add to a nail to stop it becoming rusty?

27 How would you make a spinning top from a round piece of cardboard and the stub of a pencil?

28 What would be a simple test to see which piece of cloth out of a number of pieces, would fade the most?

29 How could you test a number of strips of cloth to see which one would stretch the most?

30 How would you make a glove puppet out of a sock?

One mark for each correct answer
Total: 30
Level 3: 1–10
Level 4: 11–20
Level 5: 21–30

History

Level 3

1 Who invaded Britain under Julius Caesar in AD55?

2 Who were the Druids?

3 What did the Emperor Hadrian build across Britain?

4 What did Boudicca do?

5 What was a *forum*?

6 What was a *milestone*?

7 Which two tribes attacked from the North of Britain?

8 Who was the mythical king who was said to have fought for the Celts against the Saxons in the west country?

9 Why did Pope Gregory send Augustine to Britain?

10 In which town in Kent did Augustine and his monks settle?

Level 4

11 Which three countries did the Vikings come from?

12 What were the names of their ships?

13 What did they have carved on the front of their vessels?

14 Who was the one-eyed chief god of the Vikings?

15 What was a Viking *saga*?

16 Who was the king of Wessex who defeated the Vikings?

17 What was the Danelaw?

18 What was the great river in Egypt which flooded every year?

19 What was the name of the great tombs built for the dead leaders of Egypt?

20 What was a *pharaoh*?

Level 5

21 What was the Egyptian god *Ra* the god of?

22 What was a *priest*?

23 What was *papyrus*?

24 What happened at Troy?

25 What was a Greek *hoplite*?

26 What was the *Acropolis*?

27 Who was Hippocrates?

28 What happened at Marathon?

29 Which Greek city-state became the greatest city in the Western world?

30 What great sporting event, still in existence, began in ancient Greece?

One mark for each correct answer
Total: 30
Level 3: 1–10
Level 4: 11–20
Level 5: 21–30

Geography

Level 3
1 What is a rainforest?

2 What is the sign of an umbrella on a weather chart likely to mean?

3 Describe each of these:
(a) a hill   *(b)* a valley   *(c)* a volcano

4 Name any four cereals

5 What is the *course* of a river?

Level 4
6 What is a *capital* city?

7 What is a *crop*?

8 What is *air pollution*?

9 What is an *oil-rig*?

10 Name three different kinds of *fuel*.

11 What is a *flood*?

12 What is the main ingredient of bread?

13 What is ground or crushed to provide coffee?

Level 5

14 What is *free-range* farming?

15 What is *factory* farming?

16 Name one of the main countries where tea is grown.

17 What is butter made from?

18 What is a *nomad*?

19 What is an *oasis*?

20 Name a great desert in North Africa.

21 What happens to a metal when it is *smelted*?

22 What name is given to the top surface of the Earth?

23 How is soil formed?

One mark for each correct answer
Total: 30
Level 3: 1–10
Level 4: 11–20
Level 5: 21–30

Art, music and physical education

Because so many practical tests are involved it is not really possible for most parents to check in any detail at home the progress that their children are making in these subjects. However, by the end of Year 6 there are certain bench-marks of ability for Level 4 in all these subjects. If your child's ability seems far in excess of these, then it is a fair bet that she has reached a higher standard than the average for her age, which is Level 4.

Art

The child:

- is familiar with examples of Art from other eras and cultures;
- has been given chances to examine and discuss examples of modern Art;
- can compare these examples with her own work in certain areas, for example, still-life, landscapes, portraits, etc.;
- can use her knowledge of Art to good effect in planning and improving her own work;
- can use a number of techniques and implements in her own work, including pen and pencil drawings, paints, basket-work, collages, dyes, engraving, finger-painting, junk sculptures, masks, mosaics, papier-mâché, needlework, pastels, printing, puppets, weaving, wax crayons, textiles, etc.

Music

The child:

- can play a simple musical instrument, like a recorder or a percussion instrument;
- can understand simple musical symbols and play a part within a score;
- can perform songs with increasing control of tone quality;
- can identify different musical instruments as they are played;

- has been introduced to music of different sorts and of different eras.

Physical education

The child:

- can swim at least 25 metres;
- understands water safety;
- can memorise and repeat sequences of movements in dances and gymnastics;
- is keen to evaluate and improve her own techniques and performances in games and athletics;
- can adapt movements or dances in response to the mood of a piece of music;
- knows how to cope with her changing environment with common sense and an appreciation of the need for safety.

Test answers

Spelling

1 ground, white, flakes, cold, snowman, mouth, head, snowballs, tired, home
2 hungry, time, food, thought, grown, looked, high, reach, angry, really
3 fought, attack, destroy, behind, sailed, wheels, dragged, soldiers, night, captured

Reading

1 matches, 2 no, 3 night, 4 struck matches, 5 Christmas tree, 6 grandmother, 7 the whole box (all), 8 she died, 9 among snowdrifts. 10 Give credit for any sensible title.
11 crocodile, 12 take a stick and poke him, 13 stroke him, 14 upon the Nile, 15 river, 16 gets thinner, 17 dinner, 18 amusing, 19 pay no attention to

YEAR 6 – AGES TEN TO ELEVEN

20 9, Bridge Ave, **21** 34587, **22** Peter Blanding, **23** Tim Brayford, **24** 26, Town St, **25** 14, Cherry Walk, **26** Mary Black, **27** John Bird, **28** Tim Brayford, **29** alphabetical

Mathematics

1 68, 96, 81, 51, 97
2 78, 328, 376, 418, 493
3 43, 72
4 *(a)* 4.00, *(b)* 1.30, *(c)* 6.45, *(d)* 5.00, *(e)* 3.45, *(f)* 2.30
5 *(a)* 15 degrees, *(b)* 5 degrees

6 1 2 3 5 6 10 15 30.
7 *(a)* 459, *(b)* 864, *(c)* 138
8 8300
9 9
10 6
11 7.55 a.m.
12 *(a)* 22, *(b)* 4, *(c)* 8, *(d)* 5, *(e)* 3

13 144, 288, 315, 174
14 39110
15 *(a)* 1962, *(b)* 1792, *(c)* 5103, *(d)* 5472
16 21
17 *(a)* 20.7, *(b)* 28.9, *(c)* 16.8, *(d)* 239, *(e)* 141.2
18 *(a)* 5, *(b)* 15, *(c)* 5, *(d)* 20, *(e)* 15

Science

(If you have time you can ask your child to provide practical answers to relevant questions, carrying out experiments etc., under your strict supervision. Otherwise she can just answer the questions in a 'pen and pencil' test.)

1 It was attractive.
2 It could be cut into thin coverings.

3 They baked it in the sun.

4 (*a*) suspension, (*b*) beam, (*c*) arch

5 The movement of the Earth around the Sun.

6 Any four from: Mars, Venus, Mercury, Jupiter, Pluto, Earth, Neptune, Uranus, Saturn.

7 It is reflected from the Sun.

8 Give two marks for a diagram showing a pendulum swinging from a fixed point.

9 carbon dioxide

10 oxygen

11 igneous, metamorphic, sedimentary

12 Once-living things compressed and hardened by pressure.

13 twigs, leaves, mud

14 migration

15 Its beak.

16 A simple substance not mixed with anything else.

17 rays

18 dissolving

19 freezing

20 Any five from: marble, limestone, slate, sandstone, chalk, granite, etc.

21 electricity

22 circuit

23 Something which allows electricity to flow through it.

24 rust

25 The paper will catch fire.

26 You can see through it.

27 Give five marks for a diagram showing water turning into water vapour in heat of sun and going up from seas, rivers etc. into atmosphere, gathering as clouds and returning as rain.

28 Water turning into gas when subjected to heat.

29 Power which does work, drives machines, etc.

30 vibrations

YEAR 6 – AGES TEN TO ELEVEN

31 vocal chords
32 Tiny living things, too small to see.
33 They can turn food bad.
34 They can be used to make foods like yoghurt.
35 fungi
36 yeast
37 Freezing, drying, storing in airtight containers, etc.
38 The area over which the magnet can attract objects to it.
39 Soak up.
40 The action of weather on buildings, etc.

Design and technology

(Again, if you have time, your child could try to design and make practical models, under your supervision, as well as providing written replies, but do not try to solder anything in response to Question 9 below – this is a theoretical question!)

1 A circular, moving object used as the basis for transport.
2 A bar used for moving something heavy.
3 A sloping object.
4 Use it again, sometimes for another purpose.
5 A sort of doll which can be moved in different ways – by strings, putting a hand inside, etc.
6 To turn a screw by inserting the edge in the top of the screw.
7 Tear paper into small pieces, soak it in water, paste it to a base.
8 Put it together.
9 Use hot, soft metal with a tool to stick pieces of metal together.
10 Copy it by pencilling the outline on to the transparent paper.

11 An object which measures time by the shadows cast by the sun.
12 Covering and protecting something.
13 Plan it in detail before starting work.

14 Reducing something to a soft liquid mass.

15 Thread the string through the holes in the reels, knotting the string at both ends to prevent slipping. Decorate the reels.

16 Take the lid off one end of each can. Thread the string between the cans. One child talk into the exposed end of one can, the other child listen through the exposed end of the other can.

17 Put some hard, small objects, like dried peas, in a container, and seal and decorate it.

18 Roll the paper into a column and stick it together.

19 Place heavy objects on top of it until it collapses.

20 To allow the rain to run off.

21 Place a piece of thick paper over the trunk of a tree and rub it with a crayon to get the impression of the bark.

22 Cut the toe off a sock. Keep the edges of one end apart by putting a wire ring round the inside. Attach the other end to a pole by strings.

23 Measure distances in centimetres up from the bottom of a container. Leave container outside to catch the rain.

24 Cut narrow end off bottle and squeeze the middle of the bottle.

25 Suspend bags by handles and place the same weights in each bag, increasing weight until there is only one bag intact.

26 Paint or grease.

27 Put the stub of the pencil, point down, through a small hole in centre of the cardboard.

28 Leave them out in the sun for a long period.

29 Suspend each strip from a line. Attach the same amount of weight to the bottom of each strip.

30 Sew buttons or something similar on to the heel of the sock to represent eyes, nose and mouth. Work the head by putting a hand inside the sock.

History

1 The Romans.
2 Priests.
3 A wall.
4 Revolt against Roman rule.
5 A market place.
6 A distance marker along a Roman road.
7 Picts and Scots.
8 Arthur.
9 To bring Christianity to Britain again.
10 Canterbury.

11 Norway, Denmark, Sweden.
12 Longships.
13 Figureheads.
14 Odin.
15 A story, or legend.
16 Alfred.
17 An area of Britain in which Alfred allowed the Danes to live.
18 The Nile.
19 Pyramids.
20 An Egyptian ruler.

21 The sun.
22 A religious leader, a servant of the gods.
23 A form of paper made from reeds.
24 The Greeks laid siege to the city.
25 A soldier.
26 A sacred area for temples.
27 A doctor, one of the founders of medical science.
28 The Greeks defeated the Persians in battle.
29 Athens.
30 The Olympic Games.

Geography

1 A wet tropical forest, with trees growing thickly together.
2 Rain.
3 *(a)* A raised piece of land, smaller than a mountain.
  (b) Low-lying ground between hills.
  (c) A mountain which has in the past erupted or exploded, or sometimes still erupts.
4 Wheat, barley, rye, maize, etc.
5 The route it follows

6 The chief city of a country.
7 Something grown for food.
8 Fumes or unpleasant gases in the air.
9 An installation from which oil is pumped.
10 Coal, electricity, gas, solar heating, etc.
11 A rush of water.
12 Flour.
13 Beans.

14 Animals kept under free, open conditions.
15 Animals reared in large quantities in confined spaces.
16 Any one of: India, Sri Lanka, China.
17 Cream.
18 A wanderer
19 A fertile spot in a desert.
20 The Sahara.
21 It is melted in order to separate ingredients.
22 The crust.
23 Over a period of time from crumbling rocks.

Parents talking

❝ *The only real disaster was a home–school National Curriculum project on Health Education. There was too much of a credibility gap for it ever to succeed. The school doctor was better known as Butcher, and it was rumoured that the school nurse wrestled under an assumed name at the local drill-hall.* ❞

❝ *I had been away for a few days and had lost touch with school events. It came as a bit of a surprise when I went in to collect my son at the end of the week and found the headmaster standing in the corridor, wearing a cowboy hat and costume and with a six-shooter in a holster around his waist. I thought, "I knew it! He's been going off for a long time and now he's finally flipped!" Actually it turned out to be a fund-raising exercise, where everybody could wear silly clothes to school if they paid some money into the school fund. All the same, they were a nasty few minutes when I first saw the man standing there mournfully, looking like an ageing Billy the Kid.* ❞

❝ *I don't regard myself as a particularly sentimental sort of person but I was weeping on the last day of my son's time at his primary school. It had been such a happy place, with teachers, parents and children all working together so well. I knew then that I would never be as fully involved in my son's education again, or get as close to his all-round development.* ❞

Index

INDEX